Mrs. Warren's Profession

GEORGE BERNARD SHAW

COSIMOCLASSICS

NEW YORK

Mrs. Warren's Profession was originally published in 1893.

Library of Congress Cataloging-in-Publication Data
A catalog record for this book is available from the Library of Congress

Cover design by www.kerndesign.net

ISBN: 1-59605-980-X

People are always blaming their circumstances for what they are. I don't believe in circumstances. The people who get on in this world are the people who get up and look for the circumstances they want, and, if they can't find them, make them.

——from Act II

CAST
(In order of appearance.)

Mr. Praed

Miss Vivie Warren

Mrs. Kitty Warren

Sir George Crofts

Mr. Frank Gardner

The Reverend Samuel Gardner

ACTS

ACT 1. A cottage garden, summer afternoon.

ACT 2. Inside the cottage, that same evening.

ACT 3. Rectory garden, next morning.

ACT 4. Honoria Fraser's chambers, Saturday.

ACT 1

Summer afternoon in a cottage garden on the eastern slope of a hill a little south of Halsemere in Surrey. Looking up the hill, the cottage is seen at the lefthand corner of the garden, with its thatched roof and porch, and a large latticed window to the left of the porch. Farther back a little wing is built out, making an angle with the right side wall. From the end of this wing a paling curves across and forward, completely shutting in the garden, except for a gate on the right. The common rises uphill beyond the paling to the skyline. Some folded canvas garden chairs are leaning against the side bench in the porch. A lady's bicycle is propped against the wall, under the window. A little to the right of the porch a hammock is slung between two posts. A big canvas umbrella, stuck in the ground, keeps the sun off the hammock, in which a young lady lies reading and making notes, her head toward the cottage and her feet toward the gate. In front of the hammock, and within reach of her hand, is a common chair, with a pile of serious-looking books and a supply of writing paper upon it.

A gentleman walking on the common comes into sight from behind the cottage. He is hardly past middle age, with something of the artist about him, unconventional but carefully dressed, and clean-shaven except for a moustache, with an eager, susceptible face and very amiable and considerate manners. He has silky black hair, with waves of grey and white in it. His eyebrows are white, his moustache black. He seems uncertain of his way. He looks over the paling, takes stock of the place, and sees the young lady.

THE GENTLEMAN. *(Taking off his hat.)* I beg your pardon. Can you direct me to Hindhead View—Mrs. Alison's?

THE YOUNG LADY. *(Glancing up from her book.)* This is Mrs. Alison's. *(She resumes her work.)*

THE GENTLEMAN. Indeed! Perhaps...may I ask, are you Miss Vivie Warren?

THE YOUNG LADY. *(Sharply, as she turns on her elbow to get a good look at him.)* Yes.

7

THE GENTLEMAN. *(Daunted and conciliatory.)* I'm afraid I appear intrusive. My name is Praed. *(Vivie at once throws her book upon the chair and gets out of the hammock.)* Oh, pray don't let me disturb you.

VIVIE. *(Striding to the gate and opening it for him.)* Come in, Mr. Praed. *(He comes in.)* Glad to see you. *(She offers her hand and takes his with a resolute and hearty grip. She is an attractive specimen of the sensible, highly-educated young middle-class Englishwoman. Age 22. Prompt, strong, confident, self-possessed. Plain, business-like dress, but not dowdy. She wears a chatelaine at her belt, with a fountain pen and a paper knife among its pendants.)*

PRAED. Very kind of you indeed, Miss Warren. *(She shuts the gate with a vigorous slam; he passes in to the middle of the garden, exercising his fingers, which are slightly numbed by her greeting.)* Has your mother arrived?

VIVIE. *(Quickly, evidently sensing aggression.)* Is she coming?

PRAED. *(Surprised.)* Didn't you expect us?

VIVIE. No.

PRAED. Now goodness me, I hope I've not mistaken the day. That would be just like me, you know. Your mother arranged that she was to come down from London and that I was to come over from Horsham to be introduced to you.

VIVIE. *(Not at all pleased.)* Did she? Hm! My mother has rather a trick of taking me by surprise...to see how I behave myself when she's away, I suppose. I fancy I shall take my mother very much by surprise one of these days, if she makes arrangements that concern me without consulting me beforehand. She has not arrived.

PRAED. *(Embarrassed.)* I'm really very sorry.

VIVIE. *(Throwing off her displeasure.)* It's not your fault, Mr. Praed, is it? And I'm very glad you've come, believe me. You are the only one of my mother's friends I have asked her to bring to see me.

PRAED. *(Relieved and delighted.)* Oh, now this is really very good of you, Miss Warren!

VIVIE. Will you come indoors, or would you rather sit out here while we talk?

PRAED. It will be nicer out here, don't you think?

VIVIE. Then I'll go and get you a chair. *(She goes to the porch for a garden chair.)*

PRAED. *(Following her.)* Oh, pray, pray! Allow me! *(He lays hands on the chair.)*

VIVIE. *(Letting him take it.)* Take care of your fingers; they're rather dodgy things, those chairs. *(She goes across to the chair with the books on it, pitches them into the hammock, and brings the chair forward with one swing.)*

PRAED. *(Who has just unfolded his chair.)* Oh, now do let me take that hard chair! I like hard chairs.

VIVIE. So do I. *(She sits down.)* Sit down, Mr. Praed. *(This invitation she gives with genial peremptoriness, his anxiety to please her clearly striking her as a sign of weakness of character on his part.)*

PRAED. By the way, though, hadn't we better go to the station to meet your

8

mother?

VIVIE. *(Very coolly.)* Why? She knows the way. *(Praed hesitates, and then sits down in the garden chair, rather disconcerted.)* Do you know, you are just like what I expected. I hope you are disposed to be friends with me.

PRAED. *(Again beaming.)* Thank you , my dear Miss Warren; thank you. Dear me! I'm so glad your mother hasn't spoiled you.

VIVIE. How?

PRAED. Well, in making you too conventional. You know, my dear Miss Warren, I am a born anarchist. I hate authority. It spoils the relations between parent and child...even between mother and daughter. Now I was always afraid that your mother would strain her authority to make you very conventional. It's such a relief to find that she hasn't.

VIVIE. Oh! Have I been behaving unconventionally?

PRAED. Oh, no; oh, dear, no. At least not conventionally unconventionally, you understand. *(She nods. He goes on, with a cordial outburst.)* But it was so charming of you to say that you were disposed to be friends with me! You modern young ladies are splendid...perfectly splendid!

VIVIE. *(Dubiously.)* Eh? *(Watching him with dawning disappointment as to the quality of his brains and character.)*

PRAED. When I was your age, young men and women were afraid of each other; there was no good fellowship...nothing real...only gallantry copied out of novels, and as vulgar and affected as it could be. Maidenly reserve! Gentlemanly chivalry! Always saying no when you meant yes! Simple purgatory for shy and sincere souls!

VIVIE. Yes, I imagine there must have been a frightful waste of time...especially women's time.

PRAED. Oh, waste of life, waste of everything. But things are improving. Do you know, I have been in a positive state of excitement about meeting you ever since your magnificent achievements at Cambridge...a thing unheard of in my day. It was perfectly splendid, your tieing with the third wrangler. Just the right place, you know. The first wrangler is always a dreamy, morbid fellow, in whom the thing is pushed to the length of a disease.

VIVIE. It doesn't pay. I wouldn't do it again for the same money.

PRAED. *(Aghast.)* The same money!

VIVIE. I did it for fifty pounds. Perhaps you don't know how it was. Mrs. Latham, my tutor at Newnham, told my mother I could distinguish myself in the mathematical tripos if I went in for it in earnest. The papers were full just then of Phillipa Summers beating the senior wrangler...you remember about it, and nothing would please my mother but that I should do the same thing. I said flatly that it was not worth my while to face the grind since I was not going in for teaching, but I offered to try for fourth wrangler or thereabouts for fifty pounds. She closed with me at that, after a little grumbling, and I was better than my bargain. But I wouldn't do it again for that. Two hundred pounds would have been nearer the mark.

PRAED. *(Much damped.)* Lord bless me! That's a very practical way of looking at it.

VIVIE. Did you expect to find me an unpractical person?

9

PRAED. No, no. But surely it's practical to consider not only the work these honors cost, but also the culture they bring.

VIVIE. Culture! My dear Mr. Praed, do you know what the mathematical tripos means? It means grind, grind, grind, for six to eight hours a day at mathematics, and nothing but mathematics. I'm supposed to know something about science, but I know nothing except the mathematics it involves. I can make calculations for engineers, electricians, insurance companies and so on, but I know next to nothing about engineering or electricity or insurance. I don't even know arithmetic well. Outside mathematics, lawn-tennis, eating, sleeping, cycling and walking, I'm a more ignorant barbarian than any woman could possibly be who hadn't gone in for the tripos.

PRAED. *(Revolted.)* What a monstrous, wicked, rascally system! I knew it! I felt at once that it meant destroying all that makes womanhood beautiful.

VIVIE. I don't object to it on that score in the least. I shall turn it to very good account, I assure you.

PRAED. Pooh! In what way?

VIVIE. I shall set up in chambers in the City and work at actuarial calculations and conveyancing. Under cover of that I shall do some law, with one eye on the Stock Exchange all the time. I've come down here by myself to read law...not for a holiday, as my mother imagines. I hate holidays.

PRAED. You make my blood run cold. Are you to have no romance, no beauty in your life?

VIVIE. I don't care for either, I assure you.

PRAED. You can't mean that.

VIVIE. Oh, yes, I do. I like working and getting paid for it. When I'm tired of working, I like a comfortable chair, a cigar, a little whisky, and a novel with a good detective story in it.

PRAED. *(In a frenzy of repudiation.)* I don't believe it. I am an artist, and I can't believe it; I refuse to believe it *(Enthusiastically.)* Ah, my dear Miss Warren, you haven't discovered yet, I see, what a wonderful world art can open up to you.

VIVIE. Yes, I have. Last May I spent six weeks in London with Honoria Fraser. Mamma thought we were doing a round of sightseeing together, but I was really at Honoria's chambers in Chancery Lane every day, working away at actuarial calculations for her, and helping her as well as a greenhorn could. In the evenings we smoked and talked, and never dreamed of going out except for exercise. And I never enjoyed myself more in my life. I cleared all my expenses, and got initiated into the business without a fee into the bargain.

PRAED. But bless my heart and soul, Miss Warren, do you call that trying art?

VIVIE. Wait a bit. That wasn't the beginning. I went up to town on an invitation from some artistic people in Fitzjohn's Avenue; one of the girls was a Newnham chum. They took me to the National Gallery, to the Opera, and to a concert where the band played all evening...Beethoven and Wagner and so on. I wouldn't go through that experience again for anything you could offer me. I held out for civility's sake until the third day, and then I said, plump out, that I couldn't stand any more of it, and went off to Chancery Lane. Now you know the sort of perfectly splendid modern young lady I am. How do you think I shall get on with my mother?

PRAED. *(Startled.)* Well, I hope...er...

VIVIE. It's not so much what you hope as what you believe, that I want to know.

PRAED. Well, frankly, I am afraid your mother will be a little disappointed. Not from any shortcoming on your part...I don't mean that. But you are so different from her ideal.

VIVIE. What is her ideal like?

PRAED. Well, you must have observed, Miss Warren, that people who are dissatisfied with their own bringing-up generally think that the world would be all right if everybody were to be brought up quite differently. Now your mother's life has been...er...I suppose you know...

VIVIE. I know nothing. *(Praed is appalled. His consternation grows as she continues.)* That's exactly my difficulty. You forget, Mr. Praed, that I hardly know my mother. Since I was a child I have lived in England, at school or college, or with people paid to take charge of me. I have been boarded out all my life, and my mother has lived in Brussels or Vienna and never let me go to her. I only see her when she visits England for a few days. I don't complain; it's been very pleasant, for people have been very good to me, and there has always been plenty of money to make things smooth. But don't imagine I know anything about my mother. I know far less than you do.

PRAED. *(Very ill at ease.)* In that case... *(He stops, quite at a loss. Then, with a forced attempt at gaiety.)* But what nonsense we are talking! Of course you and your mother will get on capitally. *(He rises and looks abroad at the view.)* What a charming little place you have here!

VIVIE. *(Unmoved.)* If you think you are doing anything but confirming my worst suspicions by changing the subject like that, you must take me for a much greater fool than I hope I am.

PRAED. Your worst suspicions! Oh, pray don't say that. Now don't.

VIVIE. Why won't my mother's life bear being talked about?

PRAED. Pray think, Miss Vivie. It is natural that I should have a certain delicacy in talking to my old friend's daughter about her behind her back. You will have plenty of opportunity of talking to her about it when she comes. *(Anxiously.)* I wonder what is keeping her.

VIVIE. No, she won't talk about it, either. *(Rising.)* However, I won't press you. Only, mind this, Mr. Praed. I strongly suspect there will be a battle royal when my mother hears of my Chancery Lane project.

PRAED. *(Ruefully.)* I'm afraid there will.

VIVIE. I shall win the battle, because I want nothing but my fare to London to start there tomorrow earning my own living by devilling for Honoria. Besides, I have no mysteries to keep up, and it seems she has. I shall use that advantage over her, if necessary.

PRAED. *(Greatly shocked.)* Oh, no! No, pray. You would not do such a thing.

VIVIE. Then tell me why not.

PRAED. I really cannot. I appeal to your good feeling. *(She smiles at his sentimentality.)* Besides, you may be too bold. Your mother is not to be trifled with when she is angry.

VIVIE. You can't frighten me, Mr. Praed. In that month at Chancery Lane I had opportunities of taking the measure of one or two women very like my mother, who came to consult Honoria. You may back me to win. But if I hit harder in my ignorance than I need, remember that it is you who refuse to enlighten me. Now, let us drop the subject. *(She takes her chair and replaces it near the hammock with the same vigorous swing as before.)*

PRAED. *(Taking a desperate resolution.)* One word, Miss Warren. I had better tell you. It's very difficult, but...

(Mrs. Warren and Sir George Crofts arrive at the gate. Mrs. Warren is a woman between 40 and 50, good-looking, showily dressed in a brilliant hat and a gay blouse fitting tightly over her bust and flanked by fashionable sleeves. Rather spoiled and domineering, but, on the whole, a genial and fairly presentable old blackguard of a woman.
Crofts is a tall, powerfully-built man of about 50, fashionable dressed in the style of a young man. Nasal voice, reedier than might be expected from his strong frame. Clean-shaven, bulldog jaws, large flat ears, and thick neck, gentlemanly combination of the most brutal types of city man, sporting man, and man about town.)

VIVIE. Here they are. *(Coming to them as they enter the garden.)* How do, Mother. Mr. Praed's been here this half hour, waiting for you.

MRS. WARREN. Well, if you've been waiting here, Praddy, it's your own fault; I thought you would have had the gumption to know I was coming by the 3:10 train. Vivie, put your hat on, dear; you'll get sunburned. Oh, I forgot to introduce you. Sir George Crofts...my little Vivie.

(Crofts advances to Vivie with his most courtly manner. She nods, but makes no motion to shake hands.)

CROFTS. May I shake hands with a young lady whom I have known, for a very long time, by reputation, as the daughter of one of my oldest friends?

VIVIE. *(Who has been looking him up and down sharply.)* If you like. *(She takes his tenderly offered hand and gives it a squeeze that makes him open his eyes, then turns away and speaks to her mother.)* Will you come in, or shall I get a couple more chairs? *(She goes into the porch for chairs.)*

MRS. WARREN. *(To Vivie.)* Chairs. *(To Crofts.)* Well, George, what do you think of her?

CROFTS. *(Ruefully.)* She has a powerful fist. Did you shake hands with her, Praed?

PRAED. Yes; it will pass off presently.

CROFTS. I hope so. *(Vivie reappears with two more chairs. He hurries to her assistance.)* Allow me.

MRS. WARREN. *(Patronizingly.)* Let Sir George help you with the chairs, dear.

VIVIE. *(Almost pitching the two into his arms.)* Here you are. *(She dusts her hands and turns to Mrs. Warren.)* You'd like some tea, wouldn't you?

MRS. WARREN. *(Sitting in Praed's chair and fanning herself.)* I'm dying for a drop to drink.

VIVIE. I'll see about it. *(She goes into the cottage. Sir George has by this time managed to unfold a chair and plant it beside Mrs. Warren, on her left. He throws the other on the grass and sits down, looking dejected and rather foolish, with the handle of his stick in his mouth. Praed, still very uneasy, fidgets about the garden on their right.)*

MRS. WARREN. *(To Praed, looking at Crofts.)* Just look at him, Praddy; he looks cheerful, don't he? He's been worrying my life out these three years to have that little girl of mine shown to him, and now that I've done it, he's quite out of countenance. *(Briskly.)* Come! Sit up, George, and take your stick out of your mouth. *(Crofts sulkily obeys.)*

PRAED. I think, you know...if you don't mind my saying so....that we had better get out of the habit of thinking of her as a little girl. You see she has really distinguished herself, and I'm not sure, from what I have seen of her, that she is not older than any of us.

MRS. WARREN. *(Greatly amused.)* Only listen to him, George! Older than any of us! Well, she has been stuffing you nicely with her importance.

PRAED. But young people are particularly sensitive about being treated in that way.

MRS. WARREN. Yes, and young people have to get all that nonsense taken out of them, and a good deal more, besides. Don't you interfere, Praddy. I know how to treat my own child as well as you do. *(Praed, with a grave shake of his head, walks up the garden with his hands behind his back. Mrs. Warren pretends to laugh, but looks after him with perceptible concern. Then she whispers to Crofts.)* What is the matter with him? Why does he seem to take it like that?

CROFTS. *(Morosely.)* You're afraid of Praed.

MRS. WARREN. What! Me! Afraid of dear old Praddy! Why, a fly wouldn't be afraid of him.

CROFTS. You're afraid of him.

MRS. WARREN. *(Angry.)* I'll trouble you to mind your own business and not try any of your sulks on me. I'm not afraid of you, anyhow. If you can't make yourself agreeable, you'd better go home. *(She gets up, and, turning her back on him, finds herself face to face with Praed.)* Come, Praddy, I know it was only your tender-heartedness. You're afraid I'll bully her.

PRAED. My dear Kitty, you think I'm offended. Don't imagine that...pray don't. But you know I often notice things that escape you, and though you never take my advice, you sometimes admit afterward that you ought to have taken it.

MRS. WARREN. Well, what do you notice now?

PRAED. Only that Vivie is a grown woman. Pray, Kitty, treat her with every respect.

MRS. WARREN. *(With genuine amazement.)* Respect! Treat my own daughter with respect! What will you think of next!

VIVIE. *(Appearing at the cottage door and calling to Mrs. Warren.)* Mother, will you come up to my room and take your bonnet off before tea?

MRS. WARREN. Yes, dearie. *(She laughs indulgently at Praed and pats him on the cheek as she passes him on his way to the porch. She follows Vivie into the cottage.)*

CROFTS. *(Furtively.)* I say, Praed.

PRAED. Yes.

CROFTS. I want to ask you a rather particular question.

PRAED. Certainly. *(He takes Mrs. Warren's chair and sits close to Crofts.)*

CROFTS. That's right; they might hear us from the window. Look here; did Kitty ever tell you who that girl's father is?

PRAED. Never.

CROFTS. Have you any suspicion of who it might be?

PRAED. None.

CROFTS. *(Not believing him.)* I know, of course, that you perhaps might feel bound not to tell if she had said anything to you. But it's very awkward to be uncertain about it now that we shall be meeting the girl every day. We don't know exactly how we ought to feel toward her.

PRAED. What difference can that make? We take her on her own merits. What does it matter who her father was?

CROFTS. *(Suspiciously.)* Then you know who he was?

PRAED. *(With a touch of temper.)* I said no just now. Did you not hear me?

CROFTS. Look here, Praed. I ask you as a particular favor. If you do know... *(Movement of protest from Praed.)* ...I only say, if you know, you might at least set my mind at rest about her. The fact is, I feel attracted toward her. Oh, don't be alarmed; it's quite an innocent feeling. That's what puzzles me about it. Why, for all I know, I might be her father.

PRAED. You! Impossible! Oh, no, nonsense!

CROFTS. *(Catching him up cunningly.)* You know for certain that I'm not?

PRAED. I know nothing about it, I tell you, any more than you. But really, Crofts... Oh, no, it's out of the question. There's not the least resemblance.

CROFTS. As to that, there's no resemblance between her and her mother that I can see. I suppose she's not your daughter, is she?

PRAED. *(He meets the question with an indignant stare, then recovers himself with an effort and answers gently and gravely.)* Now listen to me, my dear Crofts. I have nothing to do with that side of Mrs. Warren's life, and never had. She has never spoken to me about it, and of course I have never spoken to her about it. Your delicacy will tell you that a handsome woman needs some friends who are not...well, not on that footing with her. The effect of her own beauty would become a torment to her if she could not escape from it occasionally. You are probably on much more confidential terms with Kitty than I am. Surely you can ask her the question yourself.

CROFTS. *(Rising impatiently.)* I have asked her, often enough. But she's so determined to keep the child all to herself that she would deny it ever had a father if she could. No, there's nothing to be got out of her...nothing that one can believe, anyhow. I'm thoroughly uncomfortable about it, Praed.

PRAED. *(Rising also.)* Well, as you are, at all events, old enough to be her

14

father, I don't mind agreeing that we both regard Miss Vivie in a parental way, as a young girl whom we are bound to protect and help. All the more, as the real father, whoever he was, was probably a blackguard.

CROFTS. *(Aggressively.)* I'm no older than you, if you come to that.

PRAED. Yes, you are, my dear fellow; you were born old. I was born a boy; I've never been able to feel the assurance of a grown-up man in my life.

MRS. WARREN. *(Calling from within the cottage.)* Prad-dee! George! Tea-ea-ea-ea!

CROFTS. *(Hastily.)* She's calling us. *(He hurries in. Praed shakes his head bodingly, and is following slowly when he is hailed by a young gentleman who has just appeared on the common and is making for the gate. He is a pleasant, pretty, smartly dressed, and entirely good-for-nothing young fellow, not long turned 20, with a charming voice and agreeably disrespectful manners. He carries a very light sporting magazine rifle.)*

THE YOUNG GENTLEMAN. Hallo! Praed!

PRAED. Why, Frank Gardner! *(Frank comes in and shakes hands cordially.)* What on earth are you doing here?

FRANK. Staying with my father.

PRAED. The Roman father?

FRANK. He's rector here. I'm living with my people this autumn for the sake of economy. Things came to a crisis in July; the Roman father had to pay my debts. He's stony broke in consequence, and so am I. What are you up to in these parts? Do you know the people here?

PRAED. Yes, I'm spending the day with a Miss Warren.

FRANK. *(Enthusiastically.)* What! Do you know Vivie? Isn't she a jolly girl! I'm teaching her to shoot...you see! *(Showing the rifle.)* I'm so glad she knows you; you're just the sort of fellow she ought to know. *(He smiles, and raises the charming voice almost to a singing tone as he exclaims.)* It's ever so jolly to find you here, Praed. Isn't it now?

PRAED. I'm an old friend of her mother's. Mrs. Warren brought me over to make her daughter's acquaintance.

FRANK. The mother! Is she here?

PRAED. Yes...inside, at tea.

MRS. WARREN. *(Calling from within.)* Prad-dee-ee-ee-eee! The tea-cake'll be cold!

PRAED. *(Calling.)* Yes, Mrs. Warren. In a moment. I've just met a friend here.

MRS. WARREN. A what?

PRAED. *(Louder.)* A friend.

MRS. WARREN. Bring him up.

PRAED. All right. *(To Frank.)* Will you accept the invitation?

FRANK. *(Incredulous, but immensely amused.)* Is that Vivie's mother?

PRAED. Yes.

FRANK. By Jove! What a lark! Do you think she'll like me?

PRAED. I've no doubt you'll make yourself popular, as usual. Come in and try. *(Moving toward the house.)*

FRANK. Stop a bit. *(Seriously.)* I want to take you into my confidence.

PRAED. Pray don't. It's only some fresh folly, like the barmaid at Redhill.

FRANK. It's ever so much more serious than that. You say you've only just met Vivie for the first time?

PRAED. Yes.

FRANK. *(Rhapsodically.)* Then you can have no idea what a girl she is. Such character! Such sense! And her cleverness! Oh, my eye, Praed, but I can tell you she is clever! And the most loving little heart that...

CROFTS. *(Putting his head out of the window.)* I say, Praed. What are you about? Do come along. *(He disappears.)*

FRANK. Hallo! Sort of chap that would take a price at a dog show, isn't he? Who's he?

PRAED. Sir George Crofts, an old friend of Mrs. Warren's. I think we had better go in.

(On their way to the porch they are interrupted by a call from the gate. Turning, they see an elderly clergyman looking over it.)

THE CLERGYMAN. *(Calling.)* Frank!

FRANK. Hallo! *(To Praed.)* The Roman Father. *(To the clergyman.)* Yes, gov'nor...all right...presently. *(To Praed.)* Look here, Praed. You'd better go in to tea. I'll join you directly.

PRAED. Very good. *(He raises his hat to the clergyman, who acknowledges the salute distantly. Praed goes into the cottage. The clergyman remains stiffly outside the gate, with his hands on the top of it. The Reverend Samuel Gardner, a beneficed clergyman of the Established Church, is over 50. He is a pretentious, booming, noisy person, hopelessly asserting himself as a father and a clergyman without being able to command respect in either capacity.)*

REVEREND SAMUEL. Well, sir. Who are your friends here, if I may ask?

FRANK. Oh, it's all right, governor! Come in.

REVEREND SAMUEL. No, sir, not until I know whose garden I am entering.

FRANK. It's all right. It's Miss Warren's.

REVEREND SAMUEL. I have not seen her at Church since she came.

FRANK. Of course not; she's a third wrangler...ever so intellectual!...took a higher degree than you did, so why should she go to hear you preach?

REVEREND SAMUEL. Don't be disrespectful, sir.

FRANK. Oh, it don't matter; nobody hears us. Come in. *(He opens the gate, unceremoniously pulling his father with it into the garden.)* I want to introduce you to her. She and I get on rattling well together; she's charming. Do you remember the advice you gave me last July, gov'nor?

REVEREND SAMUEL. *(Severely.)* Yes. I advised you to conquer your idleness and flippancy, and to work your way into an honourable profession and live on it and not upon me.

FRANK. No, that's what you thought of afterward. What you actually said was that since I had neither brains nor money, I'd better turn my good looks to account by marrying somebody with both. Well, look here. Miss Warren has brains; you can't deny that.

REVEREND SAMUEL. Brains are not everything.

FRANK. No, of course not; there's the money...

REVEREND SAMUEL. *(Interrupting him austerely.)* I was not thinking of money, sir. I was speaking of higher things...social position, for instance.

FRANK. I don't care a rap about that.

REVEREND SAMUEL. But I do, sir.

FRANK. Well, nobody wants you to marry her. Anyhow, she has what amounts to a high Cambridge degree, and she seems to have as much money as she wants.

REVEREND SAMUEL. *(Sinking into a feeble vein of humor.)* I greatly doubt whether she has as much money as you will want.

FRANK. Oh, come; I haven't been so very extravagant. I live ever so quietly; I don't drink, I don't bet much, and I never go regularly on the razzle-dazzle as you did when you were my age.

REVEREND SAMUEL. *(Booming hollowly.)* Silence, sir.

FRANK. Well, you told me yourself, when I was making ever such an ass of myself about the barmaid at Redhill, that you once offered a woman fifty pounds for the letters you wrote to her when...

REVEREND SAMUEL. *(Terrified.)* Sh-sh-sh, Frank, for Heaven's sake! *(He looks around apprehensively. Seeing no one within earshot, he plucks up courage to boom again, but more subdued.)* You are taking an ungentlemanly advantage of what I confided to you for your own good, to save you from an error you would have repented all your life long. Take warning by your father's follies, sir, and don't make them an excuse for your own.

FRANK. Did you ever hear the story of the Duke of Wellington and his letters?

REVEREND SAMUEL. No, sir, and I don't want to hear it.

FRANK. The Old Iron Duke didn't throw away fifty pounds...not he. He just wrote, "My dear Jenny: Publish and be Damned! Yours affectionately, Wellington." That's what you should have done.

REVEREND SAMUEL. *(Piteously.)* Frank, my boy, when I wrote those letters, I put myself into that woman's power. When I told you about her I put myself, to some extent, I am sorry to say, in your power. She refused my money with these words, which I shall never forget: "Knowledge is power," she said, "and I never sell power." That's more than twenty years ago, and she has never made use of her power or caused me a moment's uneasiness. You are behaving worse to me than she did, Frank.

FRANK. Oh, yes, I dare say! Did you ever preach at her the way you preach at me every day?

REVEREND SAMUEL. *(Wounded almost to tears.)* I leave you, sir. You are incorrigible. *(He turns toward the gate.)*

FRANK. *(Utterly unmoved.)* Tell them I shan't be home to tea, will you, gov'nor, like a good fellow? *(He goes toward the cottage door and is met by Vivie coming out, followed by Praed, Crofts and Mrs. Warren.)*

VIVIE. *(To Frank.)* Is that your father, Frank? I do so want to meet him.

FRANK. Certainly. *(Calling after his father.)* Gov'nor! *(The Reverend Samuel turns at the gate, fumbling nervously at his hat. Praed comes down the garden on the opposite side, beaming in anticipation of civilities. Crofts prowls about near the hammock, poking it with his stick to make it swing. Mrs. Warren halts at the threshold, staring hard at the clergyman.)* Let me introduce...my father; Miss Warren.

VIVIE. *(Going to the clergyman and shaking his hand.)* Very glad to see you here, Mr. Gardner. Let me introduce everybody. Mr. Gardner...Mr. Frank Gardner...Mr. Praed...Sir George Crofts, and... *(As the men are raising their hats to one another, Vivie is interrupted by an exclamation from her mother, who swoops down on the Reverend Samuel.)*

MRS. WARREN. Why, it's Sam Gardner, gone into the church! Don't you know us, Sam? This is George Crofts, as large as life and twice as natural. Don't you remember me?

REVEREND SAMUEL. *(Very red.)* I really...er...

MRS. WARREN. Of course you do. Why, I have a whole album of your letters still; I came across them only the other day.

REVEREND SAMUEL. *(Miserably confused.)* Miss Vavasour, I believe.

MRS. WARREN. *(Correcting him quickly in a loud whisper.)* Tch! Nonsense...Mrs. Warren. Don't you see my daughter there?

CURTAIN

ACT 2

Inside the cottage after nightfall. Looking eastward from within instead of westward from without, the latticed window, with its curtains drawn, is now seen in the middle of the front wall of the cottage, with the porch door to the left of it. In the lefthand side wall is the door leading to the wing. Farther back against the same wall is a dresser with a candle and matches on it, and Frank's rifle standing beside them, with the barrel resting in the plate-rack. In the center a table stands with a lighted lamp on it. Vivie's books and writing materials are on a table to the right of the window, against the wall. The fireplace is on the right, with a settle; there is no fire. Two of the chairs are set right and left of the table.

The cottage door opens, showing a fine starlit night without, and Mrs. Warren, her shoulders wrapped in a shawl borrowed from Vivie, enters, followed by Frank. She has had enough of walking, and gives a gasp of relief as she unpins her hat, takes it off, sticks the pin through the crown, and puts it on the table.

MRS. WARREN. O Lord! I don't know which is the worst of the country, the walking or the sitting at home with nothing to do. I could do a whiskey and soda now, if only they had such a thing in this place.

FRANK. *(Helping her to take off her shawl, and giving her shoulders the most delicate possible little caress with his fingers as he does so.)* Perhaps Vivie's got some.

MRS. WARREN. *(Glancing back at him for an instant from the corner of her eye as she detects the pressure.)* Nonsense! What would a young girl like her be doing with such things! Never mind, it don't matter. *(She throws herself wearily into a chair at the table.)* I wonder how she passes her time here! *(Looking about.)* I'd rather be in Vienna.

FRANK. Let me take you there. *(He folds the shawl neatly, hangs it on the back of the other chair, and sits down opposite Mrs. Warren.)*

MRS. WARREN. Get out! I'm beginning to think you're a chip off the old block.

FRANK. Like the gov'nor, eh?

MRS. WARREN. Never you mind. What do you know about such things? You're only a boy.

FRANK. Do come to Vienna with me? It would make a wonderful time.

MRS. WARREN. No, thank you. Vienna is no place for you...at least not until you're a little older. *(She nods at him to emphasise this piece of advice. He makes a mock-piteous face, belied by his laughing eyes. She looks at him, then rises and goes to him.)* Now look here, little boy... *(Taking his face in her hands and turning it up to her.)* ...I know you through and through by your likeness to your father, better than you know yourself. Don't you go taking any silly ideas into your head about me.

FRANK. *(Gallantly wooing her with his voice.)* Can't help it, my dear Mrs. Warren; it runs in the family. *(She pretends to box his ears, then looks at the pretty, laughing, upturned face for a moment, tempted. At last she kisses him and immediately turns away, out of patience with herself.)*

MRS. WARREN. There! I shouldn't have done that. I am wicked. Never mind, my dear; it's only a motherly kiss. Go and make love to Vivie.

FRANK. So I have.

MRS. WARREN. *(Turning on him with a sharp note of alarm in her voice.)* What!

FRANK. Vivie and I are very close friends.

MRS. WARREN. What do you mean? Now see here...I won't have any young scamp tampering with my little girl. Do you hear? I won't have it.

FRANK. *(Quite unabashed.)* My dear Mrs. Warren, don't you be alarmed. My intentions are honourable...ever so honourable, and your little girl is jolly well able to take care of herself. She doesn't need looking after half so much as her mother. She's not a beauty queen.

MRS. WARREN. *(Taken aback by his assurance.)* Well, you have got a nice, healthy two inches of cheek all over you. I don't know where you got it...not from your father, anyhow. *(Voices and footsteps in the porch.)* Sh! I hear the others coming in. *(She sits down hastily.)* Remember, you've got your warning. *(The Reverend Samuel comes in, followed by Crofts.)* Well, what became of you two? And where's Praddy and Vivie?

CROFTS. *(Putting his hat on the settle and his stick in the chimney corner.)* They went up the hill. We went to the village. I wanted a drink. *(He sits down on the settle, putting his legs up along the seat.)*

MRS. WARREN. Well, she shouldn't go off like that without telling me. *(To Frank.)* Get your father a chair, Frank; where are your manners? *(Frank springs up and gracefully offers his father his chair, then takes another from the wall and sits down at the table, in the middle, with his father on his right and Mrs. Warren on his left.)* George, where are you going to stay tonight? You can't stay here. And what's Praddy going to do?

CROFTS. Gardner'll put me up.

MRS. WARREN. Oh, no doubt you've taken care of yourself! But what about Praddy?

CROFTS. Don't know. I suppose he can sleep at the inn.

MRS. WARREN. Haven't you room for him, Sam?

REVEREND SAMUEL. Well, er...you see, as rector here, I am not free to do as I like exactly. Er...what is Mr. Praed's social position?

MRS. WARREN. Oh, he's all right; he's an architect. What an old stick-in-the-mud you are, Sam!

FRANK. Yes, it's all right, gov'nor. He built that place down in Monmouthshire for the Duke of Beaufort...Tintern Abbey, they call it. You must have heard of it. *(He winks with lightning smartness at Mrs. Warren and regards his father blandly.)*

REVEREND SAMUEL. Oh, in that case, we shall only be too happy , I suppose he knows the Duke of Beaufort personally.

FRANK. Oh, ever so intimately! We can stick him in Georgina's old room.

MRS. WARREN. Well, that's settled. Now if those two would only come in and let us have supper. They've no right to stay out after dark like this.

CROFTS. *(Aggressively.)* What harm are they doing you?

MRS. WARREN. Well, harm or not, I don't like it.

FRANK. Better not wait for them, Mrs. Warren. Praed will stay out as long as possible. He has never known before what it is to stray over the heath on a summer night with my Vivie.

CROFTS. *(Sitting up in consternation.)* I say, you know. Come!

REVEREND SAMUEL. *(Startled out of his professional manner into real force and sincerity.)* Frank, once and for all, it's out of the question. Mrs. Warren will tell you that it's not to be thought of.

CROFTS. Of course not.

FRANK. *(With enchanting placidity.)* Is that so, Mrs. Warren?

MRS. WARREN. *(Reflectively.)* Well, Sam, I don't know. If the girl wants to get married, no good can come of keeping her unmarried.

REVEREND SAMUEL. *(Astounded.)* But married to him!...your daughter to my son! Only think; it's impossible.

CROFTS. Of course it's impossible. Don't be a fool, Kitty.

MRS. WARREN. *(Nettled.)* Why not? Isn't my daughter good enough for your son?

REVEREND SAMUEL. But surely, my dear Mrs. Warren, you know the reason...

MRS. WARREN. *(Defiantly.)* I know no reasons. If you know any, you can tell them to the lad, or to the girl, or to your congregation, if you like.

REVEREND SAMUEL. *(Helplessly.)* You know very well I couldn't tell anyone the reasons. But my boy will believe me when I tell him there are reasons.

FRANK. Quite right, Dad; he will. But has your boy's conduct ever been influenced by your reasons?

CROFTS. You can't marry her, and that's all about it. *(He gets up and stands on the hearth, with his back to the fireplace, frowning determinedly.)*

MRS. WARREN. *(Turning on him sharply.)* What have you got to do with it, pray?

FRANK. *(With his prettiest lyrical cadence.)* Precisely what I was going to ask, myself, in my own graceful fashion.

CROFTS. *(To Mrs. Warren.)* I suppose you don't want to marry the girl to a man younger than herself and without either a profession or a few pennies to keep her on. Ask Sam, if you don't believe me. *(To the Reverend Samuel.)* How much more money are you going to give him?

REVEREND SAMUEL. Not another penny. He has had his patrimony, and he spent the last of it in July. *(Mrs. Warren's face falls.)*

CROFTS. *(Watching her.)* There! I told you. *(He resumes his place on the settle and puts up his legs on the seat again, as if the matter were finally disposed of.)*

FRANK. *(Plaintively.)* This is ever so mercenary. Do you suppose Miss Warren's going to marry for money? If we love one another...

MRS. WARREN. Thank you. Your love's a pretty cheap commodity, my lad. If you have no means of keeping a wife, that settles it; you can't have Vivie.

FRANK. *(Much amused.)* What do you say, gov'nor, eh?

REVEREND SAMUEL. I agree with Mrs. Warren.

FRANK. And good old Crofts has already expressed his opinion.

CROFTS. *(Turning angrily on his elbow.)* Look here...I want none of your cheek.

FRANK. *(Pointedly.)* I'm ever so sorry to surprise you, Crofts, but you allowed yourself the liberty of speaking to me like a father a moment ago. One father is enough, thank you.

CROFTS. *(Contemptuously.)* Yah! *(He turns away again.)*

FRANK. *(Rising.)* Mrs. Warren. I cannot give my Vivie up, even for your sake.

MRS. WARREN. *(Muttering.)* Young scamp!

FRANK. *(Continuing.)* And as you no doubt intend to hold out other prospects to her, I shall lose no time in placing my case before her. *(They stare at him, and he begins to declaim gracefully.)*

> He either fears his fate too much,
> Or his deserts are small,
> That dares not put it to the touch
> To gain or lose it all.

(The cottage door opens while he is reciting and Vivie and Praed come in. He breaks off. Praed puts his hat on the dresser. There is an immediate improvement in the company's behaviour. Crofts takes down his legs from the settle and pulls himself together as Praed joins him at the fireplace. Mrs. Warren loses her ease of manner and takes refuge in querulousness.)

MRS. WARREN. Wherever have you been, Vivie?

VIVIE. *(Taking off her hat and throwing it carelessly on the table.)* On the hill.

MRS. WARREN. Well, you shouldn't go off like that without letting me know. How could I tell what had become of you...and night coming on, too!

VIVIE. *(Going to the door of the inner room and opening, ignoring her mother.)* Now, about supper? We shall be rather crowded in here, I'm afraid.

MRS. WARREN. Did you hear what I said, Vivie?

VIVIE. *(Quietly.)* Yes, Mother. *(Reverting to the supper difficulty.)* How

22

many are we? *(Counting.)* One, two, three, four, five, six. Well, two will have to wait until the rest are done; Mrs. Allison has only plates and knives for four.

PRAED. Oh, it doesn't matter about me. I...

VIVIE. You have had a long walk and are hungry, Mr. Praed. You shall have your supper at once. I can wait myself. I want one person to wait with me. Frank, are you hungry?

FRANK. Not the least in the world...completely off my peck, in fact.

MRS. WARREN. *(To Crofts.)* Neither are you, George. You can wait.

CROFTS. Oh, hang it, I've eaten nothing since tea-time. Can't Sam do it?

FRANK. Would you starve my poor father?

REVEREND SAMUEL. *(Testily.)* Allow me to speak for myself, sir. I am perfectly willing to wait.

VIVIE. *(Decisively.)* There's no need. Only two are wanted. *(She opens the door of the inner room.)* Will you take my mother in, Mr. Gardner. *(The Reverend Samuel takes Mrs. Warren, and they pass into the next room. Praed and Crofts follow. All except Praed clearly disapprove of the arrangement, but do not know how to resist it. Vivie stands at the door looking in at them.)* Can you squeeze past to that corner, Mr. Praed. It's rather a tight fit. Take care of your coat against the white-wash...that's right. Now, are you all comfortable?

PRAED. *(Within.)* Quite, thank you.

MRS. WARREN. *(Within.)* Leave the door open, dearie. *(Frank looks at Vivie, then steals to the cottage door and softly sets it wide open.)* Oh Lord, what a draught! You'd better shut it, dear. *(Vivie shuts it promptly. Frank noiselessly shuts the cottage door.)*

FRANK. *(Exulting.)* Aha! Got rid of 'em. Well, Vivums, what do you think of my governor?

VIVIE. *(Preoccupied and serious.)* I've hardly spoken to him. He doesn't strike me as being a particularly able person.

FRANK. Well, you know, the old man is not altogether such a fool as he looks. You see, he's rector here, and in trying to live up to it, he makes a much bigger ass of himself than he really is. No, the governor ain't so bad, poor old chap, and I don't dislike him as much as you might expect. He means well. How do you think you'll get on with him?

VIVIE. *(Rather grimly.)* I don't think my future life will be much concerned with him, or with any of that old circle of my mother's, except perhaps Praed. What do you think of my mother?

FRANK. Really and truly?

VIVIE. Yes, really and truly.

FRANK. Well, she's ever so jolly. But she's rather a caution, isn't she? And Crofts? Oh, my eye, Crofts!

VIVIE. What a lot, Frank!

FRANK. What a crew!

VIVIE. *(With intense contempt for them.)* If I thought that I was like that...that I was going to be a waster, shifting along from one meal to another with no purpose, and no character, and no grit in me, I'd open an artery and bleed to death without one moment's hesitation.

FRANK. Oh, no, you wouldn't. Why should they take any grind when they can afford not to? I wish I had their luck. No, what I object to is their form. It isn't the thing; it's slovenly, ever so slovenly.

VIVIE. Do you think your form will be any better when you're as old as Crofts, if you don't work?

FRANK. Of course I do...ever so much better. Vivums mustn't lecture...her little boy's incorrigible. *(He attempts to take her face caressingly in his hands.)*

VIVIE. *(Striking his hands down sharply.)* Off with you; Vivvums is not in a humor for petting her little boy this evening.

FRANK. How unkind!

VIVIE. *(Stamping at him.)* Be serious. I'm serious.

FRANK. Good. Let us talk learnedly. Miss Warren, do you know that all the most advanced thinkers are agreed that half the diseases of modern civilization are due to starvation of the affections in the young? Now, I...

VIVIE. *(Cutting him short.)* You are getting tiresome. *(She opens the inner door.)* Have you room for Frank there? He's complaining of starvation.

MRS. WARREN. *(Within.)* Of course there is. *(Clatter of knives and glasses as she moves things on the table.)* Here, there's room now beside me. Come along, Mr. Frank.

FRANK. *(Aside to Vivie, as he goes.)* Her little boy will be ever so even with his Vivvums for this. *(He goes into the other room.)*

MRS. WARREN. *(Within.)* Here, Vivie. Come on, you, too, child. You must be famished. *(She enters, followed by Crofts, who holds the door open for Vivie with marked deference. She goes out without looking at him, and he shuts the door after her.)* Why George, you can't be done; you've eaten nothing.

CROFTS. Oh, all I wanted was a drink. *(He thrusts his hands in his pockets and begins prowling about the room, restless and sulky.)*

MRS. WARREN. Well, I like enough to eat. But a little of that cold beef and cheese and lettuce goes a long way. *(With a sigh of only half repletion she sits down lazily at the table.)*

CROFTS. What do you go encouraging that young pup for?

MRS. WARREN. *(On the alert at once.)* Now see here, George; what are you up to about that girl? I've been watching your way of looking at her. Remember...I know you and what your looks mean.

CROFTS. There's no harm in looking at her, is there?

MRS. WARREN. I'd put you out and pack you back to London pretty soon if I saw any of your nonsense. My girl's little finger is more to me than your whole body and soul. *(Crofts receives this with a sneering grin. Mrs. Warren, flushing a little at her failure to impose on him in the character of a theatrically devoted mother, adds a lower key.)* Make your mind easy; the young pup has no more chance than you have.

CROFTS. Mayn't a man take an interest in a girl?

MRS. WARREN. Not a man like you.

CROFTS. How old is she?

MRS. WARREN. Never you mind how old she is.

CROFTS. Why do you make such a secret of it?

MRS. WARREN. Because I choose.

CROFTS. Well, I'm not fifty yet, and my property is as good as it ever was...

MRS. WARREN. *(Interrupting him.)* Yes, because you're as stingy as you're vicious.

CROFTS. And a baronet isn't to be picked up every day. No other man in my position would put up with you for a mother-in-law. Why shouldn't she marry me?

MRS. WARREN. You!

CROFTS. We three could live together quite comfortably. I'd die before her and leave her a bouncing widow with plenty of money. Why not? It's been growing in my mind all the time I've been walking with that fool inside there.

MRS. WARREN. *(Revolted.)* Yes, it's the sort of thing that would grow in your mind. *(He halts in his prowling and the two look at one another, she steadfastly, with a sort of awe behind her contemptuous disgust, he stealthily, with a carnal gleam in his eye and a loose grin, tempting her.)*

CROFTS. *(Suddenly anxious and urgent as he sees no sign of sympathy in her.)* Look here, Kitty, you're a sensible woman; you needn't put on any moral airs. I'll ask no more questions, and you need answer none. I'll settle the whole property on her, and if you want a cheque for yourself on the wedding day, you can name any figure you like...within reason.

MRS. WARREN. Faugh! So it's come to that with you, George, like all the other worn out old creatures.

CROFTS. *(Savagely.)* Damn you! *(She rises and turns fiercely on him, but the door of the inner room is opened just then, and the voices of the others are heard returning. Crofts, unable to recover his presence of mind, hurries out of the cottage. The clergyman comes backs.)*

REVEREND SAMUEL. *(Looking around.)* Where is Sir George.

MRS. WARREN. Gone out to have a pipe. *(She goes to the fireplace, turning her back on him to compose herself. The clergyman goes to the table for his hat. Meanwhile Vivie comes in, followed by Frank, who collapses into the nearest chair with an air of extreme exhaustion. Mrs. Warren looks around at Vivie and says, with her affectation of maternal patronage even more forced than usual.)* Well, dearie, have you had a good supper?

VIVIE. You know what Mrs. Alison's suppers are. *(She turns to Frank and pets him.)* Poor Frank! Was all the beef gone? Did it get nothing but bread and cheese and ginger beer? *(Seriously, as if she had done quite enough trifling for one evening.)* Her butter is really awful. I must get some down from the stores.

FRANK. Do, in Heaven's name!

(Vivie goes to the writing-table and makes a memorandum to order the butter. Praed comes in from the inner room, putting up his handkerchief, which he has been using as a napkin.)

REVEREND SAMUEL. Frank, my boy, it is time for us to be thinking of home. Your mother does not know yet that we have visitors.

PRAED. I'm afraid our stay will cause trouble.

FRANK. Not the least in the world, Praed; my mother will be delighted to see you. She's a genuinely intellectual, artistic woman, and she sees nobody here from one year's end to another except the gov'nor, so you can imagine how jolly dull it pans out for her. *(To the Reverend Samuel.)* You're not intellectual or artistic, are you, Father? So take Praed home at once, and I'll stay here and entertain Mrs. Warren. You'll pick up Crofts in the garden. He'll be excellent company for the bull-pup.

PRAED. *(Taking his hat from the dresser, and coming close to Frank.)* Come with us, Frank. Mrs. Warren has not seen Miss Vivie for some time, and we have prevented them from having a moment together yet.

FRANK. *(Quite softened, and looking at Praed with admiration.)* Of course...I forgot. Ever so thanks for reminding me. Perfect gentleman, Praddy. Always were...my ideal through life. *(He rises to go, but pauses a moment between the two older men, and puts his hand on Praed's shoulder.)* Ah, if you had only been my father instead of this unworthy old man! *(He puts his other hand on his father's shoulder.)*

REVEREND SAMUEL. *(Blustering.)* Silence, sir, silence; you are profane.

MRS. WARREN. *(Laughing heartily.)* You should keep him in better order, Sam. Goodnight. Here; take George his hat and stick with my compliments.

REVEREND SAMUEL. *(Taking them.)* Goodnight. *(They shake hands. As he passes Vivie he shakes hands with her also and bids her goodnight. Then, in booming command, to Frank.)* Come along, sir, at once. *(He goes out. Meanwhile, Frank has taken his cap from the dresser and his rifle from the rack. Praed shakes hands with Mrs. Warren and Vivie and goes out, Mrs. Warren accompanying him idly to the door and looking out after him as he goes across the garden. Frank silently begs a kiss from Vivie, but she, dismissing him with a stern glance, takes a couple of books and some paper from the writing-table, and sits down with them at the middle table, so as to have the benefit of the lamp.)*

FRANK. *(At the door, taking Mrs. Warren's hand.)* Goodnight, dear Mrs. Warren. *(He squeezes her hand. She snatches it away, her lips tightening, and looks more than half disposed to box his ears. He laughs mischievously and runs off, clapping, to the door behind him.)*

MRS. WARREN. *(Coming back to her place at the table, opposite Vivie, resigning herself to an evening of boredom now that the men are gone.)* Did you ever in your life hear anyone rattle on so? Isn't he a tease? *(She sits down.)* Now that I think of it, dearie, don't you go encouraging him. I'm sure he's a regular good-for-nothing.

VIVIE. Yes, I'm afraid poor Frank is a thorough good-for-nothing. I shall have to get rid of him, but I shall feel sorry for him, though he's not worth it, poor lad. That man Crofts does not seem to be good for much either, is he?

MRS. WARREN. *(Galled by Vivie's cool tone.)* What do you know of men, child, to talk that way about them? You'll have to make up your mind to see a good deal of Sir George Crofts, as he's a friend of mine.

VIVIE. *(Quite unmoved.)* Why? Do you expect that we shall be much together...you and I, I mean?

MRS. WARREN. *(Staring at her.)* Of course...until you're married. You're not going back to college again.

VIVIE. Do you think my way of life would suit you? I doubt it.

MRS. WARREN. Your way of life! What do you mean?

VIVIE. *(Cutting a page of her book with the paper knife on her chatelaine.)* Has it really never occurred to you, Mother, that I have a way of life like other people?

MRS. WARREN. What nonsense is this you're trying to talk? Do you want to show your independence, now that you're a great little person at school? Don't be a fool, child.

VIVIE. *(Indulgently.)* That's all you have to say on the subject, is it, Mother?

MRS. WARREN. *(Puzzled, then angry.)* Don't you keep on asking me questions like that. *(Violently.)* Hold your tongue. *(Vivie works on, losing no time, and saying nothing.)* You and your way of life, indeed! What next? *(She looks at Vivie again. No reply.)* Your way of life will be what I please, so it will. *(Another pause.)* I've been noticing these airs in you ever since you got that tripos or whatever you call it. If you think I'm going to put up with them you're mistaken, and the sooner you find it out, the better. *(Muttering.)* All I have to say on the subject, indeed! *(Again, raising her voice angrily.)* Do you know who you're speaking to, Miss?

VIVIE. *(Looking across at her without raising her head from her book.)* No. Who are you? What are you?

MRS. WARREN. *(Rising breathless.)* You young imp!

VIVIE. Everybody knows my reputation, my social standing, and the profession I intend to pursue. I know nothing about you. What is the way of life which you invite me to share with you and Sir George Crofts, pray?

MRS. WARREN. Take care. I shall do something I'll be sorry for after, and you, too.

VIVIE. *(Putting aside her books with cool decision.)* Well, let us drop the subject until you are better able to face it. *(Looking critically at her mother.)* You want some good walks and a little lawn tennis to set you up. You are shockingly out of condition; you were not able to manage twenty yards uphill today without stopping to pant, and your wrists are mere rolls of fat. Look at mine. *(She holds out her wrists.)*

MRS. WARREN. *(After looking at her helplessly, begins to whimper.)* Vivie...

VIVIE. *(Springing up sharply.)* Now pray don't begin to cry. Anything but that. I really cannot stand whimpering. I will go out of the room if you do.

MRS. WARREN. *(Piteously.)* Oh, my darling, how can you be so hard on me? Have I no rights over you as your mother?

VIVIE. Are you my mother?

MRS. WARREN. *(Appalled.)* Am I your mother! Oh, Vivie!

VIVIE. Then where are our relatives...my father...our family friends? You claim the rights of a mother: the right to call me fool and child, to speak to me as no woman in authority over me at college dare speak to me, to dictate my way of life, and to force on me the acquaintance of a brute whom anyone can see to be the most vicious sort of London man about town. Before I give myself the trouble to resist such claims, I may as well find out whether they have any real existence.

MRS. WARREN. *(Distracted, throwing herself on her knees.)* Oh, no, no. Stop, stop. I am your mother; I swear it. Oh, you can't mean to turn on me...my own child; it's not natural. You believe me, don't you? Say you believe me.

VIVIE. Who was my father?

MRS. WARREN. You don't know what you're asking. I can't tell you.

VIVIE. *(Determinedly.)* Oh, yes, you can, if you like. I have a right to know, and you know very well that I have that right. You can refuse to tell me, if you please, but if you do, you will see the last of me tomorrow morning.

MRS. WARREN. Oh, it's too horrible to hear you talk like that. You wouldn't...you couldn't leave me.

VIVIE. *(Ruthlessly.)* Yes, without a moment's hesitation, if you trifle with me about this. *(Shivering with disgust.)* How can I feel sure that I may not have the contaminated blood of that brutal waster in my veins?

MRS. WARREN. No, no. On my oath it's not he, nor any of the rest that you have ever met. I'm certain of that, at least. *(Vivie's eyes fasten sternly on her mother as the significance of this flashes on her.)*

VIVIE. You are certain of that, at least. Ah! You mean that that is all you are certain of. *(Thoughtfully.)* I see. *(Mrs. Warren buries her face in her hands.)* Don't do that, Mother; you know you don't feel it a bit. *(Mrs. Warren takes down her hands and looks up deplorably at Vivie, who takes out her watch and says.)* Well, that is enough for tonight. At what hour would you like breakfast? Is half-past eight too early for you?

MRS. WARREN. *(Wildly.)* My God, what sort of woman are you?

VIVIE. *(Coolly.)* The kind the world is mostly made of, I should hope. Otherwise I don't see how it gets its business done. Come... *(Taking her mother by the wrist and pulling her up pretty resolutely.)* ...pull yourself together. That's right.

MRS. WARREN. *(Querulously.)* You're very rough with me, Vivie.

VIVIE. Nonsense. What about bed? It's past ten.

MRS. WARREN. *(Passionately.)* What's the use of my going to bed? Do you think I could sleep?

VIVIE. Why not? I shall.

MRS. WARREN. You! You've no heart. *(She suddenly breaks out vehemently in her natural tongue...the dialect of a woman of the people...with all her affectations of maternal authority and conventional manners gone, and an overwhelming inspiration of true conviction and scorn in her.)* Oh, I won't bear it; I won't put up with the injustice of it. What right have you to set yourself up above me like this? You boast of what you are to me...to me, who gave you the chance of being what you are. What chance had I? Shame on you for a bad daughter and a stuck-up prude!

VIVIE. *(Cool and determined, but no longer confident, for her replies, which have sounded convincingly sensible and strong to her so far, now begin to ring rather woodenly and even priggishly against the new tone of her mother.)* Don't think for a moment I set myself above you in any way. You attacked me with the conventional authority of a mother; I defended myself with the conventional superiority of a respectable woman. Frankly, I am not going to stand any of your nonsense, and when you drop it, I shall not expect you to stand any of mine. I shall always respect your right to your own opinions and your own way of life.

MRS. WARREN. My own opinions and my own way of life! Listen to her talking! Do you think I was brought up like you...able to pick and choose my own way of life? Do you think I did what I did because I liked it, or thought it right, or wouldn't rather have gone to college and been a lady if I'd had the chance?

VIVIE. Everybody has some choice, Mother. The poorest girl alive may not be able to choose between being Queen of England or Principal of Newnham, but she can choose between ragpicking and flowerselling, according to her taste. People are always blaming their circumstances for what they are. I don't believe in circumstances. The people who get on in this world are the people who get up and look for the circumstances they want, and, if they can't find them, make them.

MRS. WARREN. Oh, it's easy to talk, very easy, isn't it? Here! Would you like to know what my circumstances were?

VIVIE. Yes, you had better tell me. Won't you sit down?

MRS. WARREN. Oh, I'll sit down; don't you be afraid. *(She plants her chair farther forward with brazen energy, and sits down. Vivie is impressed, in spite of herself.)* Do you know who your grandmother was?

VIVIE. No.

MRS. WARREN. No, you don't. I do. She called herself a widow and had a fried-fish shop down by the Mint, and kept herself and four daughters out of it. Two of us were sisters; that was me and Liz, and we were both good looking and well made. I suppose our father was a well-fed man; mother pretended he was a gentleman, but I don't know. The other two were only half sisters...undersized, ugly, starved looking, hard working, honest poor creatures. Liz and I would have half-murdered them if Mother hadn't half-murdered us to keep our hands off them. They were the respectable ones. Well, what did they get by their respectability? I'll tell you. One of them worked in a whitelead factory twelve hours a day for nine shillings a week until she died of lead poisoning. She only expected to get her hands a little paralyzed, but she died. The other was always held up to us as a model because she married a Government laborer in the Deptford victualling yard, and kept his room and the three children neat and tidy on eighteen shillings a week...until he took to drink. That was worth being respectable for, wasn't it?

VIVIE. *(Now thoughtfully attentive.)* Did you and you sister think so?

MRS. WARREN. Liz didn't, I can tell you; she had more spirit. We both went to a church school...that was part of the ladylike airs we gave ourselves to be superior to the children that knew nothing and went nowhere...and we stayed there until Liz went out one night and never came back. I know the schoolmistress thought I'd soon follow her example, for the clergyman was always warning me that Lizzie'd end by jumping off Waterloo Bridge. Poor fool...that was all he knew about it! But I was more afraid of the whitelead factory than I was of the river, and so would you have been in my place. That clergyman got me a situation as a scullery maid in a temperance restaurant where they sent out for anything you liked. Then I was waitress, and then I went to the bar at Waterloo station...fourteen hours a day serving drinks and washing glasses for four shillings a week and my board. That was considered a great promotion for me. Well, one cold, wretched night, when I was so tired I could hardly keep myself awake, who should come in for a half of Scotch but Lizzie, in a long fur cloak, elegant and comfortable, with a lot of sovereigns in her purse.

VIVIE. *(Grimly.)* My aunt Lizzie!

MRS. WARREN. Yes, and a very good aunt to have, too. She's living down at Winchester, now, close to the cathedral, one of the most respectable ladies there...chaperones girls at the county ball, if you please. No river for Liz, thank you! You remind me of Liz a little; she was a first-rate business woman...saved money from the beginning...never let herself look too much like what she was...never lost her head or threw away a chance. When she saw I'd grown up good looking, she said to me across the bar, "What are you doing there, you little fool? wearing out your health and your appearance for other people's profit!" Liz was saving money then to take a house for herself in Brussels, and she thought we two could save faster than one. So she loaned me some money and gave me a start, and I saved steadily and first paid her back, and then went into business with her as her partner. Why shouldn't I have done it? The house in Brussels was real high class...a much better place for a woman to be in than the factory where Anne Jane got poisoned. None of our girls were ever treated as I was treated in the scullery of that temperance place, or at the Waterloo bar, or at home. Would you have had me stay in them and become a worn out old drudge before I was forty?

VIVIE. *(Intensely interested by this time.)* No, but why did you choose that business? Saving money and good management will succeed in any business.

MRS. WARREN. Yes, saving money. But where can a woman get the money to save in any other business? Could you save out of four shillings a week and keep yourself dressed as well? Not you. Of course, if you're a plain woman and can't earn anything more, or if you have a turn for music, or the stage, or newspaper-writing, that's different. But neither Liz nor I had any turn for such things; all we had was our appearance and our turn for pleasing men. Do you think we were such fools as to let other people trade in our good looks by employing us as shopgirls, or barmaids, or waitresses, when we could trade in them ourselves and get all the profits instead of starvation wages? Not likely.

VIVIE. You were certainly quite justified...from the business point of view.

MRS. WARREN. Yes, or any other point of view. What is any respectable girl brought up to do but to catch some rich man's fancy and get the benefit of his money by marrying him?...as if a marriage ceremony could make any difference in the right or wrong of the thing! Oh, the hypocrisy of the world makes me sick! Liz and I had to work and save and calculate just like other people, elseways we should be as poor as any good-for-nothing, drunken waster of a woman that thinks her luck will last forever. *(With great energy.)* I despise such people; they've no character, and if there's a thing I hate in a woman, it's want of character.

VIVIE. Come now, Mother...frankly! Isn't it part of what you call character in a woman that she should greatly dislike such a way of making money?

MRS. WARREN. Why, of course. Everybody dislikes having to work and make money, but they have to do it all the same. I'm sure I've often pitied a poor girl, tired out and in low spirits, having to try to please some man that she doesn't care two straws for...some half-drunken fool that thinks he's making himself agreeable when he's teasing and worrying and disgusting a woman so that hardly any money could pay her for putting up with it. But she has to bear with disagreeables and take the rough with the smooth, just like a nurse in a hospital or anyone else. It's not work that any woman would do for pleasure, goodness knows, though to hear the pious people talk you would suppose it was a bed of roses.

VIVIE. Still you consider it worthwhile. It pays.

MRS. WARREN. Of course it's worthwhile to a poor girl, if she can resist temptation and is good looking and well conducted and sensible. It's far better than any other employment open to her. I always thought that shouldn't be. It can't be right, Vivie, that there shouldn't be better opportunities for women. I stick to that...it's wrong. But it's so, right or wrong, and a girl must make the best of it. But of course it's not worthwhile for a lady. If you took to it, you'd be a fool, but I should have been a fool if I'd taken to anything else.

VIVIE. *(More and more deeply moved.)* Mother, suppose we were both as poor as you were in those wretched old days; are you quite sure that you wouldn't advise me to try the Waterloo bar, or marry a laborer, or even go into the factory?

MRS. WARREN. *(Indignantly.)* Of course not. What sort of mother do you take me for? How could you keep your self-respect in such starvation and slavery? And what's a woman worth...what's life worth...without self-respect? Why am I independent and able to give my daughter a first-rate education, when other women that had just as good opportunities are in the gutter? Because I always knew how to respect myself and control myself. Why is Liz looked up to in a cathedral town? The same reason. Where would we be now if we'd minded the clergyman's foolishness? Scrubbing floors for a dollar and a half a day and nothing to look forward to but the workhouse infirmary. Don't you be led astray by people who don't know the world, my girl. The only way for a woman to provide for herself decently is for her to be good to some man that can afford to be good to her. If she's in his own station of life, let her make him marry her, but if she's far beneath him she can't expect it...why should she? It wouldn't be for her own happiness. Ask any lady in London society that has daughters, and she'll tell you the same, except that I tell you straight and she'll tell you crooked. That's all the difference.

VIVIE. *(Fascinated, gazing at her.)* My dear mother, you are a wonderful woman...you are stronger than all England. And are you really and truly not one wee bit doubtful...or...or...ashamed?

MRS. WARREN. Well, of course, dearie, it's only good manners to be ashamed of it; it's expected from a woman. Women have to pretend to feel a great deal that they don't feel. Liz used to be angry with me for plumping out the truth about it. She used to say that when every woman could learn enough from what was going on in the world before her eyes, there was no need to talk about it to her. But then Liz was such a perfect lady! She had the true instinct

31

of it, while I was always a bit of a vulgarian. I used to be so pleased when you sent me your photographs to see that you were growing up like Liz; you've just her ladylike, determined way. But I can't stand saying one thing when everyone knows I mean another. What's the use in such hypocrisy? If people arrange the world that way for women, there's no good pretending that it's arranged the other way. I never was a bit ashamed, really. I consider that I had a right to be proud that we managed everything so respectably and never had a word against us, and that the girls were so well taken care of. Some of them did very well...one of them married an ambassador. But of course now I dare not talk about such things; whatever would they think of us! *(She yawns.)* Oh, dear! I do believe I'm getting sleepy after all. *(She stretches herself lazily, thoroughly relieved by her explosion, and placidly ready for her night's rest.)*

VIVIE. I believe it is I who will not be able to sleep now. *(She goes to the dresser and lights the candle. Then she extinguishes the lamp, darkening the room a good deal.)* Better let in some fresh air before locking up. *(She opens the cottage door and finds that it is broad moonlight.)* What a beautiful night! Look! *(She draws aside the curtains of the window. The landscape is seen bathed in the radiance of the harvest moon rising over Blackdown.)*

MRS. WARREN. *(With a perfunctory glance at the scene.)* Yes, dear, but take care you don't catch your death of cold from the night air.

VIVIE. *(Contemptuously.)* Nonsense.

MRS. WARREN. *(Querulously.)* Oh, yes, everything I say is nonsense, according to you.

VIVIE. *(Turning to her quickly.)* No, really that is not so, Mother. You have got completely the better of me tonight, though I intended it to be the other way. Let us be good friends now.

MRS. WARREN. *(Shaking her head a little ruefully.)* So it has been the other way. But I suppose I must give in to it. I always got the worst of it from Liz, and now I suppose it'll be the same with you.

VIVIE. Well, never mind. Come...goodnight, dear old Mother. *(She takes her mother in her arms.)*

MRS. WARREN. *(Fondly.)* I brought you up well, didn't I, dearie?

VIVIE. You did.

MRS. WARREN. And you'll be good to your poor old mother for it, won't you?

VIVIE. I will, dear. *(Kissing her.)* Goodnight.

MRS. WARREN. *(With unction.)* Blessings on my own dearie darling...a mother's blessing! *(She embraces her daughter protectingly, instinctively looking upward as if to call down a blessing.)*

CURTAIN

ACT 3

In the Rectory garden next morning, with the sun shining and the birds in full song. The garden wall has a five-barred wooden gate, wide enough to admit a carriage, in the middle. Beside the gate hangs a bell on a coiled spring, communicating with a pull outside. The carriage drive comes down the middle of the garden and then swerves to its left, where it ends in a little gravelled circus opposite the Rectory porch. Beyond the gate is seen the dusty high road, parallel with the wall, bounded on the farther side by a strip of turf and an unfenced pine wood. On the lawn, between the house and the drive, is a clipped yew tree, with a garden bench in its shade. On the opposite side the garden is shut in by a box hedge, and there is a sundial on the turf, with an iron chair near it. A little path leads off through the box hedge, behind the sundial.

Frank, seated on the chair near the sundial, on which he has placed the morning papers, is reading the Standard. His father comes from the house, red-eyed and shivery, and meets Frank's eye with misgiving.

FRANK. *(Looking at his watch.)* Half past eleven. Nice hour for a rector to come down to breakfast!

REVEREND SAMUEL. Don't mock, Frank, don't mock. I am a little...er... *(Shivering.)*

FRANK. Off-colour?

REVEREND SAMUEL. *(Repudiating the expression.)* No, sir...unwell this morning. Where's your mother?

FRANK. Don't be alarmed; she's not here. Gone to town by the 11:13 with Bessie. She left several messages for you. Do you feel equal to receiving them now, or shall I wait till you've had breakfast?

REVEREND SAMUEL. I have had breakfast, sir. I am surprised at your mother going to town when we have people staying with us. They'll think it very strange.

FRANK. Possibly she has considered that. At all events, if Crofts is going to stay here, and you are going to sit up every night with him until four, recalling

33

the incidents of your fiery youth, it is clearly my mother's duty, as a prudent housekeeper, to go up to the stores and order a barrel of whisky and a few hundred siphons.

REVEREND SAMUEL. I did not observe that Sir George drank excessively.

FRANK. You were not in a condition to, gov'nor.

REVEREND SAMUEL. Do you mean to say that I ...

FRANK. (Calmly.) I never saw a beneficed clergyman less sober. The anecdotes you told about your past career were so awful that I really don't think Praed would have passed the night under your roof if it hadn't been for the way my mother and he took to one another.

REVEREND SAMUEL. Nonsense, sir. I am Sir George Crofts' host. I must talk to him about something; and he has only one subject. Where is Mr. Praed now?

FRANK. He is driving my mother and Bessie to the station.

REVEREND SAMUEL. Is Crofts up yet?

FRANK. Oh, long ago. He hasn't turned a hair; he's in much better practice than -you...he's kept it up ever since...probably. He's taken himself off somewhere to smoke. (Frank resumes his paper. The Reverend Samuel turns disconsolately toward the gate, then comes back irresolutely.)

REVEREND SAMUEL. Er...Frank.

FRANK. Yes.

REVEREND SAMUEL. Do you think the Warrens will expect to be asked here after yesterday afternoon?

FRANK. They've been asked here already. Crofts informed us at breakfast that you told him to bring Mrs. Warren and Vivie over here today, and to invite them to make this house their home. It was after that communication that my mother found she must go to town by the 11:13 train.

REVEREND SAMUEL. (With despairing vehemence.) I never gave any such invitation. I never thought of such a thing.

FRANK. (Compassionately.) How do you know, gov'nor, what you said and thought last night? Hallo! Here's Praed back again.

PRAED. (Coming in through the gate.) Good morning.

REVEREND SAMUEL. Good morning. I must apologise for not having met you at breakfast. I have a touch of...of...

FRANK. Clergyman's sore throat, Praed. Fortunately not chronic.

PRAED. (Changing the subject.) Well, I must say your house is in a charming spot here.

REVEREND SAMUEL. Yes, it is indeed. Frank will take you for a walk, Mr. Praed, if you like. I'll ask you to excuse me; I must take the opportunity to write my sermon while Mrs. Gardner is away and you are all amusing yourselves. You won't mind, will you?

PRAED. Certainly not. Don't stand on the slightest ceremony with me.

REVEREND SAMUEL. Thank you. I'll...er...er... (He stammers his way to the porch and vanishes into the house.)

PRAED. (Sitting down on the turf near Frank and hugging his ankles.) Curious thing it must be writing a sermon every week.

FRANK. Ever so curious, if he did it. He buys 'em. He's gone for some soda water.

PRAED. My dear boy, I wish you would be more respectful to your father. You know you can be so nice when you like.

FRANK. My dear Praddy, you forget that I have to live with the governor. When two people live together...it don't matter whether they're father and son, husband and wife, brother and sister...they can't keep up the polite humbug which comes so easy for ten minutes on an afternoon call. Now the governor, who unites to many admirable domestic qualities...the irresoluteness of a sheep and the pompousness and aggressiveness of a jackass...

PRAED. No, pray, pray, my dear Frank, remember! He is your father.

FRANK. I give him due credit for that. But just imagine his telling Crofts to bring the Warrens over here! He must have been ever so drunk. You know, my dear Praddy, my mother wouldn't stand Mrs. Warren for a moment. Vivie mustn't come here until she's gone back to town.

PRAED. But your mother doesn't know anything about Mrs. Warren, does she?

FRANK. I don't know. Her journey to town looks as if she did. Not that my mother would mind in the ordinary way; she has stuck like a brick to lots of women who had got into trouble. But they were all nice women. That's what makes the real difference. Mrs. Warren, no doubt, has her merits, but she's ever so rowdy, and my mother simply wouldn't put up with her. So...hallo! *(This exclamation is provoked by the reappearance of the clergyman, who comes out of the house in haste and dismay.)*

REVEREND SAMUEL. Frank, Mrs. Warren and her daughter are coming across the heath with Crofts; I saw them from the study windows. What am I to say about your mother?

FRANK. *(Jumping up energetically.)* Stick on your hat and go out and say how delighted you are to meet them, and that Frank's in the garden, and that mother and Bessie have been called to the bedside of a sick relative and were ever so sorry they couldn't stop, and that you hope Mrs. Warren slept well, and...and...say any blessed thing except the truth, and leave the rest to Providence.

REVEREND SAMUEL. But how are we to get rid of them afterward?

FRANK. There's no time to think of that now. Here! *(He bounds into the porch and returns immediately with a clerical felt hat, which he claps on his father's head.)* Now, off with you. Praed and I'll wait here, to give the thing an unpremeditated air. *(The clergyman, dazed but obedient, hurries off through the gate; Praed gets up from the turf, and dusts himself.)*

FRANK. We must get that old lady back to town somehow, Praed. Come! Honestly, dear Praddy, do you like seeing them together...Vivie and the old lady?

PRAED. Oh, why not?

FRANK. *(His teeth on edge.)* Doesn't it make your flesh creep ever so little?... that wicked old devil, up to every villainy under the sun, I'll swear, and Vivie...ugh!

PRAED. Hush, pray. They're coming. *(The clergyman and Crofts are seen*

35

coming along the road, followed by Mrs. Warren and Vivie walking affection- ately together.)

FRANK. Look...she actually has her arm around the old woman's waist. It's her right arm...she began it. She's gone sentimental, by God! Ugh! Ugh! Now do you feel the creeps? *(The clergyman opens the gate, and Mrs. Warren and Vivie pass him and stand in the middle of the garden looking at the house. Frank, in an ecstasy of dissimulation, turns gaily to Mrs. Warren, exclaiming.)* Ever so delighted to see you, Mrs. Warren. This quiet old rectory garden becomes you perfectly.

MRS. WARREN. Well, I never! Did you hear that, George? He says I look well in a quiet old rectory garden.

REVEREND SAMUEL. *(Still holding the gate for Crofts, who loafs through it, heavily bored.)* You look well everywhere, Mrs. Warren.

FRANK. Bravo, gov'nor! Now look here; let's have an awful jolly time of it before lunch. First let's see the church. Everyone has to do that. It's a regular old thirteenth-century church, you know; the gov'nor's ever so fond of it, because he got up a restoration fund and had it completely rebuilt six years ago. Praed will be able to show its points.

REVEREND SAMUEL. *(Mooning hospitality at them.)* I shall be please to show it if Sir George and Mrs. Warren really want to be bothered with a tour.

MRS. WARREN. Oh, come along and get it over. It'll do George good; I'll bet he doesn't do much church.

CROFTS. *(Turning back toward the gate.)* I've no objection.

REVEREND SAMUEL. Not that way. We go through the fields, if you don't mind. Around here. *(He leads the way by the little path through the box hedge.)*

CROFTS. Oh, all right. *(He goes with the parson. Praed follows with Mrs. Warren. Vivie does not stir, but watches them until they have gone, with all the lines of purpose in her face marking it strongly.)*

FRANK. Ain't you coming?

VIVIE. No. I want to give you a warning, Frank. You were making fun of my mother just now when you said that about the rectory garden. That is barred in the future. Please treat my mother with as much respect as you treat your own.

FRANK. My dear Viv, she wouldn't appreciate it. She's not like my mother; the same treatment wouldn't do for both cases. But what on earth has happened to you? Last night we were perfectly agreed as to your mother and her set. This morning I find you attitudinizing sentimentally with your arm around your parent's waist.

VIVIE. *(Flushing.)* Attitudinizing!

FRANK. That was how it struck me. First time I ever saw you do a second-rate thing.

VIVIE. *(Controlling herself.)* Yes, Frank, there has been a change, but I don't think it a change for the worse. Yesterday I was a spoiled brat.

FRANK. And today?

VIVIE. *(Wincing, then looking at him steadily.)* Today I know my mother better than you do.

36

FRANK. Heaven forbid!

VIVIE. What do you mean?

FRANK. Viv, there's a freemasonry among thoroughly immoral people that you know nothing of. You've too much character. That's the bond between your mother and me; that's why I know her better than you'll ever know her.

VIVIE. You are wrong; you know nothing about her. If you knew the circumstances against which my mother had to struggle...

FRANK. *(Adroitly finishing the sentence for her.)* ...I should know why she is what she is, shouldn't I? What difference would that make? Circumstances or no circumstances, Viv, you won't be able to stand your mother.

VIVIE. *(Very angry.)* Why not?

FRANK. Because she's an old wretch, Viv. If you ever put your arm around her waist in my presence again, I'll shoot myself there and then as a protest against an exhibition which revolts me.

VIVIE. Must I choose between dropping your acquaintance and dropping my mother's?

FRANK. *(Gracefully.)* That would put the old lady at ever such a disadvantage. No, Viv, your infatuated little boy will have to stick to you in any case. But he's all the more anxious that you shouldn't make mistakes. It's no use, Viv; your mother's impossible. She may be a good sort, but she's a bad lot, a very bad lot.

VIVIE. *(Hotly.)* Frank! *(He stands his ground. She turns away and sits down on the bench under the yew tree, struggling to recover her self-command. Then she says.)* Is she to be deserted by all the world because she's what you call a bad lot? Has she no right to live?

FRANK. No fear of that, Viv; she won't ever be deserted. *(He sits on the bench beside her.)*

VIVIE. But I am to desert her, I suppose.

FRANK. *(Babyishly, lulling her and making love to her with his voice.)* Mustn't go live with her. Little family group of mother and daughter wouldn't be a success. Spoil our little group.

VIVIE. *(Falling under the spell.)* What little group?

FRANK. The babes in the wood...Vivie and little Frank. *(He slips his arm around her waist and nestles against her like a weary child.)* Let's go and get covered up with leaves.

VIVIE. *(Rhythmically, rocking him like a nurse.)* Fast asleep, hand in hand, under the trees.

FRANK. The wise little girl with her silly little boy.

VIVIE. The dear little boy with his dowdy little girl.

FRANK. Ever so peaceful, and relieved from the imbecility of the little boy's father and the questionableness of the little girl's...

VIVIE. *(Smothering the word against her breast.)* Sh-sh-sh! Little girl wants to forget all about her mother. *(They are silent for some moments, rocking one another. Then Vivie wakes up with a shock, exclaiming.)* What a pair of fools we are! Come, sit up. Gracious! Your hair. *(She smooths it.)* I wonder if all grown-up people play in that childish way when nobody is looking. I never did it when I was a child.

FRANK. Neither did I. You are my first playmate. *(He catches her hand to kiss it, but checks himself to look around first. Very unexpectedly, he sees Crofts emerging from the box hedge.)* Oh damn!

VIVIE. Why damn, dear?

FRANK. *(Whispering.)* Sh! Here's this brute Crofts. *(He sits farther away from her with an unconcerned air.)*

VIVIE. Don't be rude to him, Frank. I particularly wish to be polite to him. It will please my mother. *(Frank makes a wry face).*

CROFTS. Could I have few words with you, Miss Vivie?

VIVIE. Certainly.

CROFTS. *(To Frank.)* You'll excuse me, Gardner. They're waiting for you in the church, if you don't mind.

FRANK. *(Rising.)* Anything to oblige you, Crofts...except church. If you want anything, Vivie, ring the gate bell, and a domestic will appear. *(He goes into the house with unruffled suavity.)*

CROFTS. *(Watching him with a crafty air as he disappears, and speaking to Vivie with an assumption of being on privileged terms with her.)* He is a pleasant young fellow, Miss Vivie. Pity he has no money, isn't it?

VIVIE. Do you think so?

CROFTS. Well, what's he to do? No profession, no property. What's he good for?

VIVIE. I realise his disadvantages, Sir George.

CROFTS. *(A little taken aback at being so precisely interpreted.)* Oh, it's not that. But while we're in this world we're in it, and money's money. *(Vivie does not answer.)* Nice day, isn't it?

VIVIE. *(With A scarcely veiled contempt for this effort at conversation.)* Very.

CROFTS. *(With brutal good humor, as if he liked her pluck.)* Well, that's not what I came to say. *(Affecting frankness.)* Now listen, Miss Vivie. I'm quite aware that I'm not a young lady's man.

VIVIE. Indeed, Sir George?

CROFTS. No, and to tell you the honest truth I don't want to be, either. But when I say a thing I mean it; when I feel sentiment I feel it in earnest, and what I value I pay hard money for. That's the sort of man I am.

VIVIE. It does you great credit, I'm sure.

CROFTS. Oh, I don't mean to praise myself. I have my faults, Heaven knows, no man is more sensible of that than I am. I know I'm not perfect; that's one of the advantages of being a middle-aged man, for I'm not a young man, and I know it. But my code is a simple one and, I think, a good one. Honour between man and man, fidelity between man and woman, and no cant about this religion or that religion, but an honest belief that things are making for good on the whole.

VIVIE. *(With biting irony.)* "A power, not ourselves, that makes for righteousness," eh?

CROFTS. *(Taking her seriously.)* Oh, certainly, not ourselves, of course. You understand what I mean. *(He sits down beside her, as one who has found a kindred spirit.)* Well, now as to practical matters. You may have an idea that

I've flung my money about, but I haven't; I'm richer today than when I first came into this property. I've used my knowledge of the world to invest my money in ways that other men have overlooked, and whatever else I may be, I'm a safe man from the money point of view.

VIVIE. It's very kind of you to tell me all this.

CROFTS. Oh, very well, come, Miss Vivie. You needn't pretend you don't see what I'm driving at. I want to settle down with a Lady Crofts. I suppose you think me very blunt, eh?

VIVIE. Not at all; I am much obliged to you for being so definite and business-like. I quite appreciate the offer...the money, the position, Lady Crofts, and so on. But I think I will say no, if you don't mind. I'd rather not. *(She rises and strolls across to the sundial to get out of his immediate neighborhood.)*

CROFTS. *(Not at all discouraged, and taking advantage of the additional room left him on the seat to spread himself comfortably, as if a few preliminary refusals were part of the inevitable routine of courtship.)* I'm in no hurry. It was only just to let you know in case young Gardner should try to trap you. Leave the question open.

VIVIE. *(Sharply.)* My no is final. I won't go back from it. *(She looks authoritatively at him. He grins, leans forward with his elbows on his knees to prod with his stick at some unfortunate insect in the grass, and looks cunningly at her. She turns away impatiently.)*

CROFTS. I'm a good deal older than you...twenty-five years...a quarter of a century. I shan't live forever, and I'll take care that you shall be well off when I'm gone.

VIVIE. I am proof against even that inducement, Sir George. Don't you think you'd better take your answer? There is not the slightest chance of my altering it.

CROFTS. *(Rising, after a final slash at a daisy, and beginning to walk to and fro.)* Well, no matter. I could tell you some things that would change your mind fast enough, but I won't, because I'd rather win you by honest affection. I was a good friend to your mother; ask her whether I wasn't. She'd never have made the money that paid for your education if it hadn't been for my advice and help, not to mention the money I advanced her. There are not many men who would have stood by her as I have. I put not less than 40,000 pounds into it, from first to last.

VIVIE. *(Staring at him.)* Do you mean to say you were my mother's business partner?

CROFTS. Yes. Now just think of all the trouble and explanations it would save if we were to keep the whole thing in the family, so to speak. Ask your mother whether she'd like to have to explain all her affairs to a perfect stranger.

VIVIE. I see no difficulty, since I understand that the business is wound up and the money invested.

CROFTS. *(Stopping short, amazed.)* Wound up! Wind up a business that's paying thirty-five percent in the worst years! Not likely. Who told you that?

VIVIE. *(Her colour quite gone.)* Do you mean that it is still...? *(She stops abruptly and puts her hand on the table to support herself. Then she gets quickly to the iron chair and sits down.*) What business are you talking about?

CROFTS. Well, the fact is it's not what would be considered exactly a high-class business in my set...the county set, you know...our set it will be if you think better of my offer. Not that there's any mystery about it; don't think that. Of course you know by your mother's being in it that it's perfectly straight and honest. I've known her for many years, and I can say of her that she'd cut off her hands sooner than touch anything that was not what it ought to be. I'll tell you about it if you like. I don't know whether you've found in travelling how hard it is to find a really comfortable private hotel.

VIVIE. (*Sickened, averting her face.*) Yes, go on.

CROFTS. Well, that's all it is. Your mother has a genius for managing such things. We've got two in Brussels, one in Berlin, one in Vienna, and two in Budapest. Of course there are others besides ourselves in it, but we hold most of the capital, and your mother's indispensable as managing director. You noticed, I daresay, that she travels a good deal. But you see you can't mention such things in society. Once let out the word hotel and everybody says you keep a public-house. You wouldn't like people to say that of your mother, would you? That's why we're so reserved about it. By the bye, you'll keep it to yourself, won't you? Since it's been a secret so long, it had better remain so.

VIVIE. And this is the business you invite me to join you in?

CROFTS. Oh no. My wife shan't be troubled with business. You'll not be in it more than you've always been.

VIVIE. I always been! What do you mean?

CROFTS. Only that you've always lived on it. It paid for your education and the dress you have on your back. Don't turn up your nose at business, Miss Vivie. Where would your Newnhams and Girtons be without it?

VIVIE. (*Rising, almost beside herself.*) Take care. I know what this business is.

CROFTS. (*Starting, with a repressed oath.*) Who told you?

VIVIE. Your partner...my mother.

CROFTS. (*Black with rage.*) The old... (*Vivie looks quickly at him. He swallows the epithet and stands swearing and raging foully to himself. But he knows that his cue is to be sympathetic. He takes refuge in generous indignation.*) She ought to have had more consideration for you. I'd never have told you.

VIVIE. I think you would probably have told me when we were married; it would have been a convenient weapon to break me in with.

CROFTS. (*Quite sincerely.*) I never intended that. On my word as a gentleman, I didn't.

(*Vivie wonders at him. Her sense of the irony of his protest cools and braces her. She replies with contemptuous self-possession.*)

VIVIE. It doesn't matter. I suppose you understand that when we leave here today our acquaintance ceases.

CROFTS. Why? Is it for helping your mother?

VIVIE. My mother was a very poor woman who had no reasonable choice but to do as she did. You were a rich gentleman, and you did the same for the sake of thirty-five percent. You are a pretty common sort of scoundrel, I think. That is my opinion of you.

CROFTS. *(After a stare. Not at all displeased, and much more at his ease on these frank terms than on than on their former ceremonious ones.)* Ha, ha, ha, ha! Go it, little missie, go it; it doesn't hurt me and it amuses you. Why the devil shouldn't I invest my money that way? I take the interest on my capital like other people; I hope you don't think I dirty my own hands with the work. Come...you wouldn't refuse the acquaintance of my mother's cousin the Duke of Belgravia because some of the rents he gets are earned in queer ways. You wouldn't cut the Archbishop of Canterbury, I suppose, because the Ecclesiastical Commissioners have a few publicans and sinners among their tenants. Do you remember your Crofts scholarship at Newnham? Well, that was founded by my brother the M.P. He gets his twenty-two percent out of a factory with six hundred girls in it, and not one of them getting wages enough to live on. How d'ye suppose most of them manage? Ask your mother. And do you expect me to turn my back on thirty-five percent when all the rest are pocketing what they can, like sensible men? No such fool! If you're going to pick and choose your acquaintances on moral principles, you'd better clear out of this country, unless you want to cut yourself out of all decent society.

VIVIE. *(Conscience stricken.)* You might go on to point out that I myself never asked where the money I spent came from. I believe I am just as bad as you.

CROFTS. *(Greatly reassured.)* Of course you are, and a very good thing, too! What harm does it do after all? *(Rallying her jocularly.)* So you don't think me such a scoundrel now you come to think it over. Eh?

VIVIE. I have shared profits with you, and I admitted to you just now to the familiarity of knowing what I think of you.

CROFTS. *(With serious friendliness.)* To be sure you did. You won't find me a bad sort; I don't go in for being superfine intellectually, but I've plenty of honest human feeling, and the old Crofts breed comes out in a sort of instinctive hatred of anything low, in which I'm sure you'll sympathize with me. Believe me, Miss Vivie, the world isn't such a bad place as the croakers make out. So long as you don't fly openly in the face of society, society doesn't ask any inconvenient questions, and it makes precious short work of the cads who do. There are no secrets better kept than the secrets that everybody guesses. In the society I can introduce you to, no lady or gentleman would so far forget themselves as to discuss my business affairs or your mother's. No man can offer you a safer position.

VIVIE. *(Studying him curiously.)* I suppose you really think you're getting on famously with me.

CROFTS. Well, I hope I may flatter myself that you think better of me than you did at first.

VIVIE. *(Quietly.)* I hardly find you worth thinking about at all now. *(She rises and turns toward the gate, pausing on her way to contemplate him and say almost gently, but with intense conviction.)* When I think of the society that tolerates you, and the laws that protect you...when I think of how helpless nine out of ten young girls would be in the hands of you and my mother...the unmentionable woman and her capitalist bully...

CROFTS. *(Livid.)* Damn you!

VIVIE. You need not. I feel among the damned already.

(She raises the latch of the gate to open it and go out. He follows her and puts his hand heavily on the top bar to prevent its opening.)

CROFTS. *(Panting with fury.)* Do you think I'll put up with this from you, you young devil, you?

VIVIE. *(Unmoved.)* Be quiet. Someone will answer the bell. *(Without flinching a step, she strikes the bell with the back of her hand. It clangs harshly and he starts back involuntarily. Almost immediately Frank appears at the porch with his rifle.)*

FRANK. *(With cheerful politeness.)* Will you have the rifle, Viv, or shall I operate?

VIVIE. Frank, have you been listening?

FRANK. Only for the bell, I assure you, so that you shouldn't have to wait. I think I showed great insight into your character, Crofts.

CROFTS. For two pins I'd take that gun from you and break it across your head.

FRANK. *(Stalking him cautiously.)* Pray don't. I'm ever so careless in handling firearms. Sure to be a fatal accident, with a reprimand from the coroner's jury for my negligence.

VIVIE. Put the rifle away, Frank. It's quite unnecessary.

FRANK. Quite right, Viv. Much more sportsmanlike to catch him in a trap. *(Crofts, understanding the insult, makes a threatening movement.)* Crofts, there are fifteen cartridges in the magazine here, and I am a dead shot at the present distance and at an object of your size.

CROFTS. Oh, you needn't be afraid. I'm not going to touch you.

FRANK. Ever so magnanimous of you under the circumstances! Thank you.

CROFTS. I'll just tell you this before I go. It may interest you, since you're so fond of one another. Allow me, Mister Frank, to introduce you to your half-sister, the eldest daughter of the Reverend Samuel Gardner. Miss Vivie, your half-brother. Good morning. *(He goes out through the gates along the road.)*

FRANK. *(After a pause of stupefaction, raising the rifle.)* You'll testify before the coroner that it's an accident, Viv. *(He takes aim at the retreating figure of Crofts. Vivie seizes the muzzle and pulls it around against her breast.)*

VIVIE. Fire now. You may.

FRANK. *(Dropping his end of the rifle hastily.)* Stop! Take care. *(She lets it go. It falls on the turf.)* Oh, you've given your little boy such a turn. Suppose it had gone off...ugh! *(He sinks on the garden seat, overcome.)*

VIVIE. Suppose it had; do you think it would not have been a relief to have some sharp physical pain tearing through me?

FRANK. *(Coaxingly.)* Take it ever so easy, dear Viv. Remember...even if the rifle scared that fellow into telling the truth for the first time in his life, that only makes us the babes in the woods in earnest. *(He holds out his arms to her.)* Come and be covered with leaves again.

VIVIE. *(With a cry of disgust.)* Ah, not that, not that. You make all my flesh creep.

FRANK. Why, what's the matter?

VIVIE. Good-bye. *(She makes for the gate.)*

FRANK. *(Jumping up.)* Hallo! Stop! Viv! Viv! *(She turns in the gateway.)* Where are you going to? Where shall we find you?

VIVIE. At Honoria Fraser's chambers, 67 Chancery Lane, for the rest of my life. *(She goes off quickly in the opposite direction to that taken by Crofts.)*

FRANK. But I say...wait...dash it! *(He runs after her.)*

CURTAIN

ACT 4

Honoria Fraser's chambers in Chancery Lane. An office at the top of the New Stone Buildings, with a plate-glass window, distempered walls, electric light, and a patent stove. Saturday afternoon. The chimneys of the Lincoln's Inn and the western sky beyond are seen through the window. There is a double writing table in the middle of the room with a cigar box, ash pans, and a portable electric reading lamp almost snowed up in heaps of papers and books. This table has knee holes and chairs right and left and is very untidy. The clerk's desk, closed and tidy, with its high stool, is against the wall, near a door communication with the inner rooms. In the opposite wall is the door leading to the public corridor. Its upper panel is of opaque glass, lettered in black on the outside, "Fraser and Warren." A baize screen hides the corner between this door and the window.

(Frank, in a fashionable light-coloured coaching suit, with his stick, gloves, and white hat in his hands, is pacing up and down the office. Somebody tries the door with a key.)

FRANK. *(Calling.)* Come in. It's not locked.

(Vivie comes in, in her hat and jacket. She stops and stares at him.)

VIVIE. What are you doing here?
FRANK. Waiting to see you. I've been here for hours. Is this the way you attend to your business? *(He puts his hat and stick on the table and perches himself with a vault on the clerk's stool, looking at her with every appearance of being in a specially restless, teasing, flippant mood.)*
VIVIE. I've been away exactly twenty minutes for a cup of tea. *(She takes off her hat and jacket and hangs them up behind the screen.)* How did you get in?
FRANK. The staff had not left when I arrived. He's gone to play football on Primrose Hill. Why don't you employ a woman, and give your sex a chance?
VIVIE. What have you come for?

44

FRANK. *(Springing off the stool and coming close to her.)* Viv, let's go and enjoy the Saturday half-holiday somewhere, like the staff. What do you say to Richmond, and then a music-hall, and a jolly supper?

VIVIE. Can't afford it. I shall put in another six hours work before I go to bed.

FRANK. Can't afford it, can we? Aha! Look here. *(He takes out a handful of coins and makes them chink.)* Gold, Viv, gold!

VIVIE. Where did you get it?

FRANK. Gambling, Viv, gambling. Poker.

VIVIE. Pah! It's meaner than stealing it. No, I'm not coming. *(She sits down to work at the table, with her back to the glass door, and begins turning over the papers.)*

FRANK. *(Remonstrating piteously.)* But, my dear Viv, I want to talk to you ever so seriously.

VIVIE. Very well...sit down in Honoria's chair and talk here. I like ten minutes' chat after tea. *(He murmurs.)* No use groaning; I'm inexorable. *(He takes the opposite seat disconsolately.)* Pass that cigar box, will you?

FRANK. *(Pushing the cigar box across.)* Nasty womanly habit. Nice men don't do it any longer.

· **VIVIE.** Yes, they object to the smell in the office, and we've had to take to cigarettes. See! *(She opens the box and takes out a cigarette, which she lights. She offers him one, but he shakes his head with a wry face. She settles herself comfortably in her chair, smoking.)* Go ahead.

FRANK. Well, I want to know what you've done...what arrangements you've made.

VIVIE. Everything was settled twenty minutes after I arrived here. Honoria has found the business too much for her this year, and she was on the point of sending for me and proposing a partnership when I walked in and told her I hadn't a farthing in the world. So I installed myself and packed her off for a fortnight's holiday. What happened at Haslemere when I left?

FRANK. Nothing at all. I said you'd gone to town on particular business.

VIVIE. Well?

FRANK. Well, either they were too flabbergasted to say anything, or else Crofts had prepared your mother. Anyhow, she didn't say anything, and Crofts didn't say anything, and Praddy only stared. After tea they got up and went, and I've not seen them since.

VIVIE. *(Nodding placidly with one eye on a wreath of smoke.)* That's all right.

FRANK. *(Looking around disparagingly.)* Do you intend to stick in this confounded place?

VIVIE. *(Blowing the wreath decisively away and sitting straight up.)* Yes. These two days have given me back all my strength and self-possession. I will never take a holiday again as long as I live.

FRANK. *(With a very wry face.)* Yes! *(Trying a different approach.)* You look quite happy...and as hard as nails.

VIVIE. *(Grimly.)* Well maybe I am!

FRANK. *(Rising.)* Look here, Viv; we must have an explanation. We parted

45

the other day under a complete misunderstanding.

VIVIE. *(Putting away the cigarette.)* Well, clear it up.

FRANK. You remember what Crofts said?

VIVIE. Yes.

FRANK. That revelation was supposed to bring about a complete change in the nature of our feeling for one another. It placed us on the footing of brother and sister.

VIVIE. Yes.

FRANK. Have you ever had a brother?

VIVIE. No.

FRANK. Then you don't know what being brother and sister feels like? Now, I have lots of sisters...Jessie and Georgina and the rest. The fraternal feeling is quite familiar to me, and I assure you my feeling for you is not the least in the world like it. The girls will go their way, I will go mine, and we shan't care if we never see one another again. That's brother and sister. But as to you, I can't be easy if I have to pass a week without seeing you. That's not brother and sister. It's exactly what I felt an hour before Crofts made his revelation. In short, dear Viv, it's love's young dream.

VIVIE. *(Bitingly.)* The same feeling, Frank, that brought your father to my mother's feet. Is that it?

FRANK. *(Revolted.)* I very strongly object, Viv, to have my feelings compared to any which the Reverend Samuel is capable of harboring, and I object still more to a comparison of you to your mother. Besides, I don't believe the story. I have taxed my father with it and obtained from him what I consider tantamount to a denial.

VIVIE. What did he say?

FRANK. He said he was sure there must be some mistake.

VIVIE. Do you believe him?

FRANK. I am prepared to take his word as against Crofts'.

VIVIE. Does it make any difference? I mean in your imagination and conscience, for of course it makes no real difference.

FRANK. *(Shaking his head.)* None whatsoever to me.

VIVIE. Nor to me.

FRANK. But that is ever so surprising! I thought our whole relations were altered in your imagination and conscience, as you put it, the moment those words were out of that brute's muzzle.

VIVIE. No, it was not that. I didn't believe him. I only wish I could.

FRANK. Eh?

VIVIE. I think brother and sister would be a very suitable relation for us.

FRANK. You really mean that?

VIVIE. Yes. It's the only relation I care for, even if we could afford any other. I mean that.

FRANK. *(Raising his eyebrows like one on whom a new light has dawned, and speaking with quite an effusion of chivalrous sentiment.)* My dear Viv, why didn't you say so before? I am ever so sorry for persecuting you. I understand, of course.

VIVIE. *(Puzzled.)* Understand what?

FRANK. Oh, I'm not a fool in the ordinary sense...only in the Scriptural sense of doing all the things the wise man declared to be folly, after trying them himself on the most intensive scale. I see I am no longer Vivvum's little boy. Don't be alarmed; I shall never call you Vivvums again...at least unless you get tired of your new little boy, whoever he may be.

VIVIE. My new little boy!

FRANK. *(With conviction.)* Must be a new little boy. Always happens that way. No other way, in fact.

VIVIE. None that you know of, fortunately for you.

(Someone knocks at the door.)

FRANK. My curse upon yon caller, whoe'er he be!

VIVIE. It's Praed. He's going to Italy and wants to say good-bye. I asked him to call this afternoon. Go and let him in.

FRANK. We can continue our conversation after his departure for Italy. I'll stay awhile. *(He goes to the door and opens it.)* How are you, Praddy. Delighted to see you. Come in. *(Praed, dressed for travelling, comes in, in high spirits, excited by the beginning of his journey.)*

PRAED. How do you do, Miss Warren. *(She presses his hand cordially, though a certain sentimentality in his high spirits jars on her.)* I start in an hour from Holborn Viaduct. I wish I could persuade you to try Italy.

VIVIE. What for?

PRAED. Why, to saturate yourself with beauty and romance, of course. *(Vivie, with a shudder, turns her chair to the table, as if the work waiting for her were a consolation and support to her. Praed sits opposite to her. Frank places a chair just behind Vivie and drops lazily and carelessly into it, talking at her over his shoulder.)*

FRANK. No use, Praddy. Viv is a little Philistine. She is indifferent to my romance, and insensible to my beauty.

VIVIE. Mr. Praed, once and for all, there is no beauty and no romance in life for me. Life is what it is, and I am prepared to take it as it is.

PRAED. *(Enthusiastically.)* You will not say that if you come to Verona and on to Venice. You will cry with delight at living in such a beautiful world.

FRANK. This is most eloquent, Praddy. Keep it up.

PRAED. Oh, I assure you, I have cried...I shall cry again, I hope...at fifty! At your age, Miss Warren, you would not need to go so far as Verona. Your spirits would absolutely fly up at the mere sight of Ostend. You would be charmed with the gaiety, the vivacity, the happy air of Brussels. *(Vivie recoils.)* What's the matter?

FRANK. Hallo, Viv!

VIVIE. *(To Praed, with deep reproach.)* Can you find no better example of your beauty and romance than Brussels to talk to me about?

PRAED. *(Puzzled.)* Of course, it's very different from Verona. I don't suggest for a moment that...

VIVIE. *(Bitterly.)* Probably the beauty and romance come to much the same in both places.

PRAED. *(Completely sobered and much concerned.)* My dear Miss Warren, I... *(Looking enquiringly at Frank.)* Is anything the matter?

FRANK. She thinks your enthusiasm frivolous, Praddy. She's had ever such a serious call.

VIVIE. *(Sharply.)* Hold your tongue, Frank. Don't be silly.

FRANK. *(Calmly.)* Do you call this good manners, Praed?

PRAED. *(Anxious and considerate.)* Shall I take him away, Miss Warren? I feel sure we have disturbed you at your work. *(He is about to rise.)*

VIVIE. Sit down; I'm not ready to go to back to work yet. You both think I have an attack of nerves. Not a bit of it. But there are two subjects I want dropped, if you don't mind. One of them... *(To Frank.)* ...is love's young dream in any shape or form; the other... *(To Praed.)* ...is the romance and beauty of life, especially as exemplified by the gaiety of Brussels. You are welcome to any illusions you may have left on these subjects; I have none. If we three are to remain friends, I must be treated as a woman of business, permanently single... *(To Frank.)* ...and permanently unromantic... *(To Praed.)*.

FRANK. I also shall remain permanently single until you change your mind. Praddy, change the subject. Be eloquent about something else.

PRAED. I'm afraid there's nothing else in the world that I can talk about. The Gospel of Art is the only one I can preach. I know Miss Warren is a great devotee of the Gospel of Getting On, but we can't discuss that without hurting your feelings, Frank, since you are determined not to get on.

FRANK. Oh, don't mind my feelings. Give me some improving advice by all means; it does me ever so much good. Have another try to make a successful man of me, Viv. Come, let's have it all: energy, thrift, foresight, self-respect, character. Don't you hate people who have no character, Viv?

VIVIE. *(Wincing.)* Oh, stop, stop; let us have no more of that horrible cant. Mr. Praed, if there are really only those two gospels in the world, we had better all kill ourselves, for the same taint is in both.

FRANK. *(Looking critically at her.)* There is a touch of poetry about you today, Viv, which I've never seen before.

PRAED. *(Remonstrating.)* My dear Frank, aren't you a little unsympathetic?

VIVIE. *(Merciless to herself.)* No, it's good for me. It keeps me from being sentimental.

FRANK. *(Bantering her.)* It is a check on your strong natural propensity, isn't it?

VIVIE. *(Almost hysterical.)* Oh, yes, go on; don't spare me. I was sentimental for one moment in my life...beautifully sentimental...by moonlight, and now...

FRANK. *(Quickly.)* I say, Viv, take care. Don't give yourself away.

VIVIE. Oh, do you think Mr. Praed does not know all about my mother? *(Turning on Praed.)* You had better have told me that morning, Mr. Praed. You are very old fashioned in your delicacies, after all.

PRAED. Surely it is you who are a little old fashioned in your prejudices, Miss Warren. I feel bound to tell you, speaking as an artist, and believing that the most intimate human relationships are far beyond and above the scope of

48

the law, that though I know that your mother is an unmarried woman, I do not respect her the less on that account. I respect her more.

FRANK. *(Airily.)* Hear, hear!

VIVIE. *(Staring at him.)* Is that all you know?

PRAED. Certainly that is all.

VIVIE. Then neither of you know anything. Your guesses are innocence itself compared to the truth.

PRAED. *(Startled and indignant, preserving his politeness with an effort.)* I hope not. *(More emphatically.)* I hope not, Miss Warren. *(Frank's face shows that he does not share Praed's incredulity. Vivie utters an exclamation of impatience. Praed's chivalry droops before the conviction. He adds, slowly.)* If there is anything worse...are you sure you have the right to tell us, Miss Warren?

VIVIE. I am aware that if I had the courage I should spend the rest of my life in telling it to everybody...in stamping and branding it into them until they felt their share in its shame and horror as I feel mine. There is nothing I despise more than the wicked convention that protects these things by forbidding a woman to mention them. And yet I can't tell you. The two infamous words that describe what my mother is are ringing in my ears and struggling on my tongue, but I can't utter them; my instinct is too strong for me. *(She buries her face in her hands. The two men, astonished, stare at one another and then at her. She raises her head again desperately and takes a sheet of paper and a pen.)* Here, let me draft you a prospectus.

FRANK. Oh, she's mad. Do you hear, Viv, mad. Come, pull yourself together.

VIVIE. You shall see. *(She writes.)* "Paid up capital. Not less than forty thousand pounds standing in the name of Sir George Crofts, Baronet, the chief shareholder." What comes next? I forget. Oh yes: "Premises at Brussels, Berlin, Vienna and Budapest. Managing Director: Mrs. Warren;" and now don't let us forget her qualifications...the two words. There! *(She pushes the paper to them.)* Oh, no...don't read it...don't! *(She snatches it back and tears it to pieces, then seizes her head in her hands and hides her face on the table. Frank, who has watched the writing carefully over her shoulder, and opened his eyes very widely at it, takes a card from his pocket, scribbles a couple of words, and silently hands it to Praed, who looks at it with amazement. Frank then remorsefully stoops over Vivie.)*

FRANK. *(Whispering tenderly.)* Viv, dear, that's all right. I read what you wrote; so did Praddy. We understand. And we remain, as this leaves us at present, yours ever so devotedly. *(Vivie slowly raises her head.)*

PRAED. We do indeed, Miss Warren. I declare you are the most splendidly courageous woman I ever met. *(This sentimental compliment braces Vivie. She throws it away from her with an impatient shake and forces herself to stand up, though not without some support from the table.)*

FRANK. Don't stir, Viv, if you don't want to. Take it easy.

VIVIE. Thank you. You can always depend on me for two things, not to cry and not to faint. *(She moves a few steps toward the door of the inner rooms and stops close to Praed to say.)* I shall need much more courage than that when

I tell my mother we have come to the parting of the ways. Now I must go into the next room for a moment to make myself neat again, if you don't mind.

PRAED. Shall we go away?

VIVIE. No, I'll be back in a moment.

(She goes into the other room, Praed opening the door for her.)

PRAED. What an amazing revelation! I'm extremely disappointed in Crofts; I am indeed.

FRANK. I'm not in the least. I feel he's perfectly accounted for at last. But what a facer for me, Praddy! I can't marry her now.

PRAED. *(Sternly.)* Frank! *(The two look at one another, Frank unruffled, Praed deeply indignant.)* Let me tell you, Gardner, that if you desert her now you will behave very despicably.

FRANK. Good old Praddy! Ever chivalrous! But you mistake; it's not the moral aspect of the case...it's the money aspect. I really can't bring myself to touch the old woman's money now.

PRAED. And was that what you were going to marry her on?

FRANK. What else? I haven't any money, nor the smallest turn for making it. If I married Viv now she would have to support me, and I should cost her more than I am worth.

PRAED. But surely a clever, bright fellow like you can make something by your own brains.

FRANK. Oh, yes, a little. *(He takes out his money again.)* I made all that yesterday...in an hour and a half. But I made it in a highly speculative business. No, dear Praddy, even if Jesse and Georgina marry millionaires and the governor dies after cutting them off without a penny, I shall have only four hundred a year. And he won't die until he's three score and ten; he hasn't originality enough. I shall be on short allowance for the next twenty years. No short allowance for Viv, if I can help it. I withdraw gracefully and leave the field to the gilded youth of England. So that's settled. I shan't worry her about it; I'll just send her a little note after we're gone. She'll understand.

PRAED. *(Grasping his hand.)* Good fellow, Frank! I heartily beg your pardon. But is it really necessary not to see her again?

FRANK. Never see her again! Hang it all, be reasonable. I shall come along as often as possible, and be her brother. I cannot understand the absurd consequences you romantic people expect from the most ordinary transactions. *(A knock at the door.)* I wonder who this is. Would you mind opening the door? If it's a client, it will look more respectable than if I appeared.

PRAED. Certainly. *(He goes to the door and opens it. Frank sits down in Vivie's chair to scribble a note.)* My dear Kitty, come in, come in.

(Mrs. Warren comes in, looking apprehensively around for Vivie. She has done her best to make herself matronly and dignified. The brilliant hat is replaced by a sober bonnet, and the gay blouse covered by a costly black silk mantle. She is pitiably anxious and ill at ease...evidently panic-stricken.)

MRS. WARREN. *(To Frank.)* What! You're here, are you?

FRANK. *(Turning in his chair from his writing, but not rising.)* Here, and charmed to see you. You come like a breath of spring.

MRS. WARREN. Oh, get out with your nonsense. *(In a low voice.)* Where's Vivie? *(Frank points expressively to the door of the inner room, but says nothing. Mrs. Warren sits down suddenly and almost begins to cry. She says.)* Praddy, won't she see me, don't you think?

PRAED. My dear Kitty, don't distress yourself. Why should she not?

MRS. WARREN. Oh, you can never see why not; you're too amiable. Mr. Frank, did she say anything to you?

FRANK. *(Folding his note.)* She must see you, if... *(Very expressively.)* ...you wait until she comes in.

MRS. WARREN. *(Frightened.)* Why shouldn't I wait?

(Frank looks quizzically at her, puts his note carefully on the ink-bottle so that Vivie cannot fail to find when next she dips her pen, then rises and devotes his attention entirely to her.)

FRANK. My dear Mrs. Warren, suppose you were a sparrow...ever so tiny and pretty a sparrow hopping in the roadway...and you saw a steamroller coming in your direction, would you wait for it?

MRS. WARREN. Oh, don't bother me with your sparrows. What did she run away from Haslemere like that for?

FRANK. I'm afraid she'll tell you if you wait until she comes back.

MRS. WARREN. Do you want me to go away?

FRANK. No. I always want you to stay. But I advise you to go away.

MRS. WARREN. What! And never see her again!

FRANK. Precisely.

MRS. WARREN. *(Crying again.)* Praddy, don't let him be cruel to me. *(She hastily checks her tears and wipes her eyes.)* She'll be so angry if she sees I've been crying.

FRANK. *(With a touch of real compassion in his airy tenderness.)* You know that Praddy is the soul of kindness, Mrs. Warren. Praddy, what do you say? Go or stay?

PRAED. *(To Mrs. Warren.)* I really should be very sorry to cause you unnecessary pain, but I think perhaps you had better not wait. The fact is... *(Vivie is heard at the inner door.)*

FRANK. Sh! Too late. She's coming.

MRS. WARREN. Don't tell her I was crying. *(Vivie comes in. She stops gravely on seeing Mrs. Warren, who greets her with hysterical cheerfulness.)* Well, dearie. So here you are at last.

VIVIE. I am glad you have come; I want to speak to you. Frank, I think you said you were going.

FRANK. Yes. Will you come with me, Mrs. Warren? What do you say to a trip to Richmond, and the theatre in the evening? There is safety in Richmond. No steam roller there.

VIVIE. Nonsense, Frank. My mother will stay here.

MRS. WARREN. *(Scared.)* I don't know; perhaps I'd better go. We're disturbing you at your work.

VIVIE. *(With quiet decision.)* Mr. Praed, please take Frank away. Sit down, Mother. *(Mrs. Warren obeys helplessly.)*

PRAED. Come, Frank. Good-bye, Miss Vivie.

VIVIE. *(Shaking hands.)* Good-bye. A pleasant trip.

PRAED. Thank you; thank you. I hope so.

FRANK. *(To Mrs. Warren.)* Good-bye; you'd be better off had you taken my advice. *(He shakes hands with her. Then airily to Vivie:)* Bye-bye, Viv.

VIVIE. Good-bye. *(He goes out gaily without shaking hands with her. Praed follows. Vivie, composed and extremely grave, sits down in Honoria's chair and waits for her mother to speak. Mrs. Warren, dreading a pause, loses no time in beginning.)*

MRS. WARREN. Well, Vivie, what did you go away like that for without saying a word to me? How could you do such a thing? And what have you done to poor George? I wanted him to come with me, but he shuffled me out of it. I could see that he was quite afraid of you. Only fancy; he wanted me not to come. As if... *(Trembling.)* ...I should be afraid of you, dearie. *(Vivie's gravity deepens.)* But of course I told him it was all settled and comfortable between us, and that we were on the best of terms. *(She breaks down.)* Vivie, what's the meaning of this? *(She produces a paper from an envelope, comes to the table, and hands its across.)* I got it from the bank this morning.

VIVIE. It is my month's allowance. They sent it to me as usual the other day. I simply sent it back to be placed to your credit, and asked them to send you the lodgement receipt. In the future I shall support myself.

MRS. WARREN. *(Not daring to understand.)* Wasn't it enough? Why didn't you tell me? *(With a cunning gleam in her eye.)* I'll double it; I was intending to double it. Only let me know how much you want.

VIVIE. You know very well that has nothing to do with it. From now on, I go my own way in my own business and among my own friends. And you will go yours. *(She rises.)* Good-bye.

MRS. WARREN. *(Appalled.)* Good-bye!

VIVIE. Yes, good-bye. Come, don't let us make a useless scene; you understand perfectly well. Sir George Crofts has told me the whole business.

MRS. WARREN. *(Angrily.)* Silly old... *(She swallows an epithet and turns white at the narrowness of her escape from uttering it.)* He ought to have his tongue cut out. But I explained it all to you, and you said you didn't mind.

VIVIE. *(Steadfastly.)* Excuse me; I do mind. You explained how it came about. That does not alter it.

(Mrs. Warren, silenced for a moment, looks forlornly at Vivie, who waits like a statue, secretly hoping that the combat is over. But the cunning expression comes back into Mrs. Warren's face and she leans across the table, sly and urgent, half whispering.)

MRS. WARREN. Vivie, do you know how rich I am?

VIVIE. I have no doubt you are very rich.

MRS. WARREN. But you don't know all that that means; you're too young. It means a new dress every day; it means theatres and balls every night; it means having the pick of all the gentlemen of Europe at your feet; it means a lovely house and plenty of servants; it means the choicest of eating and drinking; it means everything you like, everything you want, everything you can think of. And what are you here? A mere drudge, toiling and moiling early and late for your bare living and two cheap dresses a year. Think it over. *(Soothingly.)* You're shocked, I know. I can enter into your feelings, and I think they do you credit, but trust me, nobody will blame you; you may take my word for that. I know what young girls are, and I know you'll think better of it when you've turned it over in your mind.

VIVIE. So that's how it's done, is it? You must have said all that to many a woman, Mother, to have it so pat.

MRS. WARREN. *(Passionately.)* What harm am I asking you to do? *(Vivie turns away contemptuously. Mrs. Warren follows her desperately.)* Vivie, listen to me; you don't understand; you've been taught wrong on purpose; you don't know what the world is really like.

VIVIE. *(Arrested.)* Taught wrong on purpose! What do you mean?

MRS. WARREN. I mean that you're throwing away all your chances for nothing. You think that people are what they pretend to be...that the way you were taught at school and college to think right and proper is the way things really are. But it's not; it's all only a pretence, to keep the cowardly, slavish, common run of people quiet. Do you want to find that out, like other women, at forty, when you've thrown yourself away and lost your chances...or won't you take it in good time now from your own mother, that loves you and swears to you that it's the truth...gospel truth? *(Urgently.)* Vivie, the big people, the clever people, the managing people, all know it. They do as I do, and think what I think. I know plenty of them. I know them to speak to, to introduce you to, to make friends of for you. I don't mean anything wrong; that's what you don't understand; your head is full of ignorant ideas about me. What do the people that taught you know about life or about people like me? When did they ever meet me, or speak to me, or let anyone tell them about me?...the fools! Would they ever have done anything for you if I hadn't paid them? Haven't I told you that I want you to be respectable? Haven't I brought you up to be respectable? And how can you keep it up without my money and my influence and Lizzie's friends? Can't you see that you're cutting your own throat as well as breaking my heart in turning your back on me?

VIVIE. I recognise the Crofts philosophy of life, Mother. I heard it all from him that day at the Gardners'.

MRS. WARREN. You think I want to force that played-out old sot on you! I don't, Vivie; on my oath I don't.

VIVIE. It would not matter if you did; you would not succeed. *(Mrs. Warren winces, deeply hurt by the implied indifference toward her affectionate intention. Vivie, neither understanding this nor concerning herself about it, goes on calmly.)* Mother, you don't know at all the sort of person I am. I don't object to Crofts more than to any other coarsely built man of his class. To tell you the truth, I rather admire him for being strong-minded enough to enjoy himself in his own way and make plenty of money instead of living the usual shooting, hunting, dining-out, tailoring, loafing life of his set merely because all the rest do it. And I'm perfectly aware that if I'd been in the same circumstances as my aunt Liz, I'd have done exactly what she did. I don't think I'm more prejudiced or strait-laced than you; I think I'm less. I'm certain I'm less sentimental. I know very well that fashionable morality is all a pretence, and that if I took your money and devoted the rest of my life to spending it fashionably, I might be as worthless and vicious as the silliest woman could possibly want to be without having a word said to me about it. But I don't want to be worthless. I shouldn't enjoy trotting about the park to advertise my dressmaker and carriage-builder, or being bored at the opera to show off a shop windowful of diamonds.

MRS. WARREN. *(Bewildered.)* But...

VIVIE. Wait a moment...I'm not done. Tell me why you continue your business now that you are independent of it. Your sister, you told me, has left all that behind her. Why don't you do the same?

MRS. WARREN. Oh, it's all very easy for Liz; she likes good society, and has the air of being a lady. Imagine me in a cathedral town! Why, the very rooks in the trees would find me out even if I could stand the dullness of it. I must have work and excitement, or I should go melancholy mad. And what else is there for me to do? The life suits me; I'm fit for it and not for anything else. If I didn't do it somebody else would, so I don't do any real harm by it. And then it brings in money, and I like making money. No, it's no use; I can't give it up...not for anybody. But you have no need to know about it? I'll never mention it. I'll keep Crofts away. I'll not trouble you much; you see I have to be constantly running about from one place to another. You'll be quit of me altogether when I die.

VIVIE. No, I am my mother's daughter. I am like you; I must have work, and must make more money than I spend. But my work is not your work, and my way not your way. We must part. It will not make much difference to us; instead of meeting one another for perhaps a few months in twenty years, we shall never meet...that's all.

MRS. WARREN. *(Her voice stifled with tears.)* Vivie, I meant to have been more with you; I did indeed.

VIVIE. It's no use, Mother; I am not to be changed by a few cheap tears and entreaties any more than you are, I dare say.

MRS. WARREN. *(Wildly.)* Oh, you call a mother's tears cheap!

VIVIE. They cost you nothing, and you ask me to give you the peace and quietness of my whole life in exchange for them. What use would my company be to you if you could get it? What have we two in common that could make either of us happy together?

MRS. WARREN. *(Lapsing recklessly into her dialect.)* We're mother and daughter. I want my daughter. I've a right to you. Who is to care for me when I'm old? Plenty of girls have taken to me like daughters and cried at leaving me, but I let them all go because I had you to look forward to. I kept myself lonely for you. You've no right to turn on me now and refuse to do your duty as a daughter.

VIVIE. *(Jarred and antagonized by the echo of the slums in her mother's voice.)* My duty as a daughter! I thought we should come to that presently. Now once and for all, Mother, you want a daughter and Frank wants a wife. I don't want a mother, and I don't want a husband. I have spared neither Frank nor myself in sending him about his business. Do you think I will spare you?

MRS. WARREN. *(Violently.)* Oh, I know the sort you are...no mercy for yourself or anyone else. I know. My experience has done that for me anyhow; I can tell the pious, canting, hard, selfish woman when I meet her. Well, keep yourself to yourself; I don't want you. But listen to this. Do you know what I would do with you if you were a baby again...aye, as sure as there's a Heaven above us?

VIVIE. Strangle me, perhaps.

MRS. WARREN. No, I'd bring you up to be a real daughter to me, and not what you are now, with your pride and your prejudices and the college education you stole from me...yes, stole; deny it if you can; what was it but stealing? I'd bring you up in my own house, so I would.

VIVIE. *(Quietly.)* In one of your own houses.

MRS. WARREN. *(Screaming.)* Listen to her! Listen to how she spits on her mother's grey hairs! Oh, may you live to have your own daughter tear and trample on you as you have trampled on me. And you will...you will. No woman ever had luck with a mother's curse on her.

VIVIE. I wish you wouldn't rant, Mother. It only hardens me. Come; I suppose I am the only young woman you ever had in your power that you did good to. Don't spoil it all now.

MRS. WARREN. Yes, Heaven forgive me, it's true, and you are the only one that ever turned on me. Oh, the injustice of it, the injustice, the injustice! I always wanted to be a good woman. I tried honest work, and I was slave-driven until I cursed the day I ever heard of honest work. I was a good mother, and because I made my daughter a good woman she turns me out as if I was a leper. Oh, if I only had my life to live over again! I'd talk to that lying clergyman in the school. From this time forth, so help me Heaven in my last hour, I'll do wrong and nothing but wrong. And I'll prosper on it.

VIVIE. Yes, it's better to choose your line and go through with it. If I had been you, Mother, I might have done as you did, but I should not have lived one life and believed in another. You are a conventional woman at heart. That is why I am bidding you good-bye now. I am right, am I not?

MRS. WARREN. *(Taken aback.)* Right to throw away all my money!

VIVIE. No, right to get rid of you. I should be a fool not to. Isn't that so?

MRS. WARREN. *(Sulkily.)* Oh, well, yes, if you come to that, I suppose you are. But Lord help the world if everybody took to doing the right thing! And now I'd better go than stay where I'm not wanted. *(She turns to the door.)*

VIVIE. *(Kindly.)* Won't you shake hands?

MRS. WARREN. *(After looking at her fiercely for a moment with a savage impulse to strike her.)* No, thank you. Good-bye.

VIVIE. *(Matter-of-factly.)* Good-bye. *(Mrs. Warren goes out, slamming the door behind her. The strain on Vivie's face relaxes, her grave expression breaks up into one of joyous content, her breath goes out in a half-sob, half-laugh of intense relief. She goes buoyantly to her place at the writing table, pushes the electric lamp out of the way, pulls over a great sheaf of papers, and is in the act of dipping her pen in the ink when she finds Frank's note. She opens it unconcernedly and reads it quickly, giving a little laugh at some quaint turn of expression in it.)* And good-bye, Frank. *(She tears the note up and tosses the pieces in the wastepaper basket without a second thought. The lights fade slowly, as she goes at her work with a plunge and soon becomes absorbed in her figures.)*

FINAL CURTAIN

COSIMO is a specialty publisher of books and publications that inspire, inform and engage readers. Our mission is to offer unique books to niche audiences around the world.

COSIMO CLASSICS offers a collection of distinctive titles by the great authors and thinkers throughout the ages. At **COSIMO CLASSICS** timeless classics find a new life as affordable books, covering a variety of subjects including: *Biographies, Business, History, Mythology, Personal Development, Philosophy, Religion and Spirituality,* and much more!

COSIMO-on-DEMAND publishes books and publications for innovative authors, non-profit organizations and businesses. **COSIMO-on-DEMAND** specializes in bringing books back into print, publishing new books quickly and effectively, and making these publications available to readers around the world.

COSIMO REPORTS publishes public reports that affect your world: from global trends to the economy, and from health to geo-politics.

FOR MORE INFORMATION CONTACT US AT
INFO@COSIMOBOOKS.COM

❋ If you are a book-lover interested in our current catalog of books.

❋ If you are an author who wants to get published

❋ If you represent an organization or business seeking to reach your members, donors or customers with your own books and publications

**COSIMO BOOKS ARE ALWAYS
AVAILABLE AT ONLINE BOOKSTORES**

_____ **VISIT COSIMOBOOKS.COM** _____
BE INSPIRED, BE INFORMED

ATE DUE

LaVergne, TN USA
19 August 2009

155287LV00002B/1/A